Lost Women of the Bible

The Women We Thought We Knew

CAROLYN CUSTIS JAMES

ZONDERVAN®

ZONDERVAN.com/
AUTHORTRACKER
follow your favorite authors

ZONDERVAN®

Lost Women of the Bible
Copyright © 2005 by Carolyn Custis James

Requests for information should be addressed to:

Zondervan, *Grand Rapids, Michigan* 49530

Library of Congress Cataloging-in-Publication Data

James, Carolyn Custis, 1948 –
    Lost women of the Bible : finding strength and significance through
their stories / Carolyn Custis James.
        p. cm.
    Includes bibliographical references.
    ISBN 978-0-310-28525-0 (softcover)
    1. Women in the Bible. 2. Christian women — Religious life. I. Title.
BS575.J36 2005
220.9'2'082 – dc22
                                      2005017705

Published in association with the literary agency of Wolgemuth & Associates, Inc.

Interior design by Beth Shagene
Interior illustrations © 2005 by Joel Spector

Printed in the United States of America

*For my daughter, Allison
with love*

CONTENTS

ACKNOWLEDGMENTS

Years ago my dad preached a series on Abraham that breathed new life into the patriarch and showed him to be more human than I had realized. The impact of that study on me (besides encouraging me in my own often bewildering walk of faith) was to show me that the people of the Bible are no different from the rest of us. My father's down-to-earth insights opened new possibilities for my own studies and enticed me to venture beyond a surface understanding of the women in the Bible and to bring my real time questions to their stories. His influence as a biblical expositor runs through this book and continues to bless and enrich my study of God's Word.

More recently, my friend Dr. Bruce K. Waltke has taken my understanding of the Old Testament to new depths. Bruce's commentary on *Genesis* (Zondervan, 2001) is a stunning eye-opener and an absolute must for anyone attempting to understand or teach this foundational book of the Bible. I am deeply indebted to his superb Old Testament scholarship in my treatment of the women of Genesis and also of Hannah.

Along the way, there have been many friends who have read drafts, offered feedback, prayed, and encouraged me as I tackled each new chapter. Special thanks to Dixie Fraley Keller, Susan Anders, Patricia Comber, Milli Jacks, Pamela Rossi Keen, and Delma Jackson who read all or part of the manuscript and offered helpful feedback. I'm grateful to Bobb and Cheryl Biehl for their thoughtful counsel and encouragement. My thanks to the women of St. Paul's Presbyterian Church in Orlando for allowing me to test-drive some of these ideas in a women's Bible study before putting them into print.

Three women have had a uniquely profound influence on this book. My mother—a true *ezer*—who, despite her daily battles with physical pain, has somehow managed to offer strength and encouragement to me. I am blessed to have such a mother. My cousin Karen Custis Wilson (who is really more like a sister) has been both an inspiration and a support. What would we do without unlimited long distance? My daughter, Allison, who will never fathom how deeply she is loved, is a constant reminder of why I'm writing. What could be more important than to offer her and young women of her generation a richer, more expansive vision of God's calling on their lives?

Many others have contributed in significant ways to this book in one way or another. Robert Wolgemuth's wisdom, encouragement, and advocacy have been invaluable to me. Jack Kuhatschek, my editor at Zondervan, has once again proven to be an indispensable ally, and I am grateful for his friendship, interaction, and support. Thanks also to Stan Gundry for continuing to believe in me and my message; to John Topliff, Lyn Cryderman, and Verne Kenney for listening and embracing this project; to Michelle Lenger for her creative contributions to the jacket and internal artwork; to Beth Shagene for the internal layout; to Angela Scheff and Jane Haradine whose editing skills made this a better book.

Thanks to those who assisted me in my research, including Dr. Elizabeth Johnson, Distinguished Professor of Theology at Fordham University, and her graduate assistant, Ann Michaud; to Rachel Maxson, doctoral student in theology at Duke Divinity School; and to the faculty and staff of Reformed Theological Seminary in Orlando, especially Dr. Mark Futato, Dean of Faculty and Professor of Old Testament, and Keely Leim of the RTS Library.

Most of all, I want to thank my husband, Frank, who has been my strongest ally throughout this entire project. I cannot imagine what it would have been like (or even if it would have been possible) to write this book without his loving partnership. On a daily basis, he proves to me the wisdom behind the biblical adage that "two are better than one." I learned from him what a Blessed Alliance is all about, long before I came across the concept in the Bible.

Introduction:
Lost

I was lost and didn't know it.

I was the pastor's daughter and literally grew up in church. "Lost" was the last word I would have used to describe myself. I belonged to Jesus. I was in the fold—one of the "found" ones. I knew my way around my Bible, felt at home in the church, and had a clear sense of my calling as a woman. I knew where I was going in life. But I got lost anyway.

The only girl in a family of four children, I, like most of my friends, was raised by loving parents to become a wife and mother. My life plan was clear. I would be the next in a long line of women devoted to husband, home, and hearth, volunteering countless hours of ministry in the church. Everything I heard and observed within the church and read in books addressed to young Christian women reinforced these ideas. Nearly all of the women I knew walked the church's center aisle and said "I do" to marriage and motherhood. This was God's purpose for women—a plan as old as the Garden of Eden—the plan he unveiled when he created Eve to be Adam's wife and helpmeet. And then I got lost.

Wedding bells didn't ring for me after four years at a Christian college. Unlike many of my friends, I graduated without an engagement ring and no prospective husband on the horizon. In my heart, I held onto the belief that marriage and family were God's destiny for me. Then one year turned into ten, and I never felt so lost.

As the decade rolled agonizingly by, I entered the workforce, earned a seminary degree, and set up an apartment for one. This wasn't the life I expected. I felt lost as a woman and bewildered about God. What had gone wrong? Had he forgotten me? I played by the rules, dated only Christians, wasn't wild or rebellious, read my Bible, prayed, and faithfully served the church. Yet, instead of building my life around a husband and children, I was on my own, protecting and providing for myself. Who was I as a woman and what was my purpose in life if I never married or had a family? Had I misread the Bible's teaching about women or was something wrong with me?

God was challenging my ideas of him, something he continues doing to this day.[1] But there was another side to my struggle that took longer for me to engage, for he was also challenging my ideas about myself with basic questions that might never have troubled me if my life had unfolded according to plan. What does it mean to be a Christian woman? Is there a right way and a wrong way (or a best way) for a woman to walk with God? What are we supposed to do when our lives don't follow the map, either because we march to the beat of a different drummer or, as in my case, things simply don't work out? Do we, as one woman put it, "miss the best life has to offer a woman"? Or, what if we marry and have children and then something goes wrong—we lose our husband or our children don't turn out right? What then? Has our womanhood fallen short?

Some might expect those questions to go away after marriage, but when I got married, they didn't. As a matter of fact, a whole new set of questions emerged. Instead of allowing me to pick up where I left off after college and settling me into the role of stay-at-home wife and mother, God worked through my husband and circumstances we faced together to challenge my paradigm even more.

My husband appreciates a fine meal as much as any man. But he wanted more of me than cooking, cleaning house, and raising kids. He wanted (he says "needed") the experience and knowledge I brought into our marriage. He sought and valued my interaction in his work, my counsel in decisions, and my collaboration in tackling the problems that came our way. He wanted a partner, not a dependent. Instead of rendering my career temporary, unnecessary, or possibly a threat, marriage gave my vocation, gifts, and contributions a new sense of mission.

During those early years of marriage, we battled against infertility and lost. God gave me marriage (albeit a little late in the game), now motherhood seemed out of reach. Fortunately what I had learned about God through my earlier struggles as a single saved me from another spiritual nosedive. I discovered later, God has more than one way of creating families. Still, according to the biblical model, I was doomed to miss out on childbirth, which many believe is the point in life when a woman experiences her highest sense of self-fulfillment. I had run head-on into one of the major threats to a woman's identity that is exacerbated, not relieved, by prevailing Christian views of how a woman finds fulfillment and meaning in life.

Many of the churches we attended were inquisitive and eager to employ Frank's gifts, but showed no interest in mine. I'm embarrassed to admit this didn't bother me at first. I thought this was how things were supposed to work. My husband was the focus of attention now, and my job was to promote and encourage his ministries. He couldn't have disagreed more. He was interested in my calling as a Christian too and challenged me to develop and use my gifts. Certainly, if we take seriously New Testament statements about the Holy Spirit giving spiritual gifts to each member of the body of Christ, then every believer who crosses the church's threshold is bearing vital gifts for our spiritual welfare.

With Frank's urging, I ventured out into new territory both in my computer career and in ministry, where I discovered gifts and abilities I didn't know I had and certainly never expected to use. I was learning, growing, and flourishing. We worked together to nurture and raise our daughter, along with tackling the challenges of work and ministry that God brought our way. Our marriage relationship was richer than anything I could have imagined. God opened amazing opportunities for us both, and we marveled (still do marvel) at how he was weaving our lives together at so many different levels.

Looking back, I wouldn't change places with anyone. Still, whenever I consult the traditional blueprint, or something someone says reminds me I'm out of step, that old lost feeling returns with force. The truth is, I'm not a typical wife, I don't have a typical family, and my marriage isn't typical either. God gave me my heart's desire—a husband and a daughter—but in ways that shook up all my preconceived Christian categories.

It is a terrible thing to admit, but I had to lose my way before realizing how many other women feel lost too. Everywhere I go I find women struggling because their lives turned out differently than they expected. What are we to do when we don't or can't fit the mold? Or when in public we look like we have perfect lives and behind closed doors it's just a sham? And what about the gifts God entrusted to us? Does he intend for us to use them or will they get us into trouble? No matter what view we take on debates over Christian womanhood, we want to know how to live faithfully as followers of Jesus Christ. We don't want to waste our lives.

A CHANGING WORLD FOR WOMEN

The ground has shifted under women today. We are not living in the world of our mothers and grandmothers. And our daughters' world will be different from ours. Like generations before us, most of us are wives and mothers. However, many of us—more than ever before—are alone, not simply through the death of a spouse but often because we never married or are divorced. Many are single parents. We are better educated and have more career opportunities than any previous generation.

As Christian women, however, we face a conundrum. When we look at what the church is saying about women in contrast to the message coming to us from contemporary culture and from circumstances we can't control, it seems that either we are out of step or the Bible is. Given the vast opportunities, demands, and realities we face, not to mention our differing gifts and personalities, the Bible's message for women seems wooden and strangely limiting. The pattern for women handed down to us in the church simply doesn't fit all sizes and shapes that women come in these days.

A whole wave of talented women who are valued and sought out in the workplace for their training, expertise, and leadership skills are walking away from the church because it seems so uninviting to them. Tragically, the message they're picking up is that the church will clip their wings and has nothing hopeful to offer them. Even those of us who stay—women deeply committed to the church—are baffled when the church doesn't always seem to make the best use of (or even show interest in) the gifts and talents we offer.

Today when we pick up our Bibles, we want to know how to be better wives and mothers. But we have other questions too. We want to know what the Bible says to those of us whose lives don't follow the traditional formula. Is there only one biblical track for women, or does God intend and take delight in our great diversity? Are women second-class citizens in God's family, or does he value us as much as he does our husbands and brothers? Does God have large purposes for his daughters, or does his Word limit our options? Is the Bible relevant for women in the third millennium, or have we outgrown its message? I am not a prophetess, but I suspect even women who do not struggle with these questions for themselves will in time be asking them (along with a lot of men) for the sake of their daughters.

THE WOMEN WE THOUGHT WE KNEW

If there's any truth to the notion that *Men Are from Mars, Women Are from Venus*, it is undoubtedly in a woman's readiness to stop and ask for directions as soon as she realizes she is lost. That so-called female instinct drove me back to the Scriptures with my questions to look again at the women in the Bible to see if they had any wisdom for me today. Changing winds of culture, long-held traditions of the church, private opinions, and impassioned arguments concerning women must, in the final analysis, yield to the authority of God's Word. Little did I expect to find that the women in the Bible felt lost too.

Admittedly, their stories (which I thought I knew as well as my own) didn't offer much help at first. Most of them seemed out of touch with my circumstances and the struggles women are facing today. These women in the Bible had some painful struggles, but unlike so many of us, their lives almost always turned out well in the end. Furthermore, their stories usually followed the wife and mother model and reinforced the idea that God prefers to do his most important work through men. Still, a lot of things weren't adding up.

Looking closer, I began to see many women who, like me, didn't fit neatly into the traditional paradigm. Strong women like Tamar, Rahab, Deborah, Jael, Priscilla, and Junia have always posed problems for interpreters because biblical writers clearly admired these women and held them up as outstanding examples of godliness even though their conduct broke with accepted convention. They were daring, took the initiative, and courageously exercised leadership, even in their interactions with men. To resolve the conflict this poses, biblical interpreters often downsize their contributions to leave a more "suitable" impression or else reclassify them as "exceptions," thereby removing their portraits from the gallery of acceptable role models for Christian women. *(handwritten: Judges 4:17,18 21,22 5:6,24)* (In the case of Jael, I must admit driving a peg through a man's head probably is not a good Christian example. But even Jael has something important to say to us and deserves more careful study.)

Upon closer inspection, I discovered many women in the Bible had trouble fitting into the wife-and-mother definition of what it means to be a woman. They clearly embraced traditional expectations and tried desperately to live within those parameters, but ultimately found it impossible. Naomi in the Old Testament and Anna in the New enjoyed ideal lives at one point, only to lose everything through the premature death of a husband. Sarah didn't become a mother until she was ninety, which was considerably worse than my experience of delayed motherhood and hardly any woman's dream. Hagar's and Esther's lives were hopelessly reconfigured—actually sacrificed—to serve someone else's agenda. Neither woman had a voice in events that trampled underfoot her private hopes and dreams.

It is not often noted, but many stories of women in the Bible make no mention of a husband or children. Although singleness was exceedingly rare in the ancient Hebrew culture, no one knows if Miriam, Mary and Martha, or Mary Magdalene ever married. In a jarring break from the culture (and without diminishing the family), the New Testament anchors a woman's identity and purpose to her relationship with Jesus rather than to her parentage, her marital status, or her children.

As I continued to study, new details emerged that brought fresh clarity to me as a woman. To my relief, I found I was traveling a well-beaten path. Women in the Bible were quite familiar with roadblocks, disappointments, and feeling lost. They knew what it was like to hit bottom when their lives veered off in unexpected directions or when they didn't seem to count for much in the eyes of others. There were honest disclosures of anger, frustration, doubts about God, and deep insecurities about themselves. Many were thrown into circumstances that took them completely out of their comfort zone and compelled them to take a stand or fight a battle they undoubtedly expected someone else (presumably a man) to handle for them. Their remarkable honesty freed me to be honest about the complexities of being a woman in a man's world and, more importantly, to be truthful regarding the state of my own heart before God.

Time after time, they put God to the test, and he displayed the greatness of his heart for women in powerful ways I'd never noticed before. Under their tutelage I learned God has a larger vision for women than I realized, a vision that encompasses the vast diversity of all of our lives and that calls us to be more. It was clear, as I believed all along, that the Bible strongly affirms our significance as wives and mothers, but I was stunned to learn God values us just as much when our lives follow other paths. Their stories gave me the freedom to embrace the life God was opening up for me.

My excitement over what I was finding was tempered by a sense of grief that the strong voices of women in the Bible are silent at a time when women inside and outside of the church are searching for answers that can withstand the pressures and challenges confronting us today. Crucial dimensions of these ancient stories have been muted, forgotten, or passed over. It made me thankful, in a strange sort of way, that I got lost and had to search for answers myself. As I studied, I discovered I was part of an exciting trend in biblical studies that is galvanizing the study of women in the Bible and recovering the Bible's lost message for women.

A NEW POINT OF VIEW

The November 8, 2003, issue of *Newsweek* reported on a significant phenomenon in biblical studies that we should have seen coming. A whole generation of women seminarians has emerged on the scene and is enriching our understanding of Scripture as they bring the female point of view to the study of the Bible. Finally years of training women in our seminaries are beginning to pay off. A new evangelical voice—a female voice—is being heard within the arena of biblical interpretation. Women are bringing different questions as well as a different point of view to the study of God's Word, and the entry of their voices, along with their solid biblical scholarship, is enriching the church's understanding of the Bible.

Many male scholars who are interacting with their female colleagues acknowledge the significance of women's contributions and have found the addition of this missing perspective stimulating to their own research. Women are pointing out aspects of the biblical text that men, who study the Bible from a male point of view, have simply not noticed. Growing numbers of men are expressing their indebtedness to the work and insights of women.

For those who greet this development with skepticism, let me say it is not without precedent. The study of God's Word has always been a cooperative effort, constantly enriched by the various perspectives that contribute to the discussion. The existence of four gospels—Matthew, Mark, Luke, and John—strongly supports the notion that there are significant advantages to multiple points of view. I experienced the benefits of another perspective when a deaf man showed me a side to Jesus that I, as a hearing person, hadn't observed. When healing a deaf man, Jesus used a simple form of sign language—the movement of his hands, facial expressions, a touch, or a sigh—to communicate what he was doing.[2] That experience made me wonder what a young American soldier stationed in Iraq saw in the Psalms as he read prayers David wrote when he was on the battlefront. Conversations with people from Third World countries, whose cultures have more in common with the ancient world of the Bible, can open up the Scriptures in breathtaking ways to those of us with a Western point of view.

Does the Bible read differently to a deaf person, a soldier, an African, a woman? Are there aspects of the Bible each observes because of their unique perspective that others miss? My father, a seasoned expositor of the Word and a major influence on my work, commented on a study I had done on a woman of the Bible by saying, "You see things I don't see." As we collaborate in our attempts to understand the Scripture, more of the fullness of God's Word comes out. This healthy and long-overdue interaction between men and women in the study of God's Word exposes the fact that even in well-worn passages of the Bible there is more to learn.

ABOUT THIS BOOK

The women you will encounter in this book are undoubtedly old friends of yours. But even in old friendships, there is always something new to discover. Our real-life questions and the insights of a female point of view breathe fresh life into old stories and bring the women of the Bible into the twenty-first century, where we need their brand of courage and wisdom. The lost women of the Bible do not need to remain lost.

Of course I faced certain unavoidable limitations in this study. The first was simply deciding which women to include. There are some glaring omissions. Mary and Martha of Bethany are missing because I treated their stories in my earlier book, *When Life and Beliefs Collide*. Naomi and Ruth are subjects of a future book devoted entirely to them. To be honest, personal preference was the heaviest factor in my choice of the women I included.

These are women I love and who have enriched my life by what they have taught me about God.

The second limitation was the need to be selective in what I wrote about each woman, a frustrating process when there is so much to say. My purpose is not to retell the familiar stories, but to focus on lost pieces of their lives and highlight their vital contributions to Christ's kingdom. These women are full of surprises. In almost every chapter, I tossed my original outline to follow leads emerging from my study that took me in surprising new directions. Some of these women tumbled off their pedestals—a painful process to watch, but also necessary if we want a realistic portrayal and not some airbrushed version of a woman to whom we can't relate. The Bible exposes their blemishes so we can see ourselves and gain a deeper sense of God's unrelenting love for his lost daughters. Some women were rehabilitated when my study uncovered stunning levels of godliness and the powerful influence of their lives on others. As I put their stories side by side in something like a simple string of beads, quite unexpectedly an overarching storyline emerged—the evolving saga of God's relationships with his daughters.

Our study begins with Eve. No matter what we think of her, she is still the source of the Bible's blueprint for women. But happily for us, even Eve has her surprises. The obscure Mrs. Noah, the poster child for lost women of the Bible, raises crucial questions we need to be asking ourselves. Sarah and Hagar often work against each other in their quest to know God's heart for them and their place in his purposes. Next, a trio of women wield astonishing influence in ever-widening circles: Tamar confronts her tribal leader; Hannah mentors Israel's last judge and helps to shape a nation; Esther exerts her influence and turns the tide in the throne room of world power. The tone shifts in the New Testament as two Marys—one from Nazareth and the other from Magdela—illumine Jesus' view of women. We will see another side of the much-maligned apostle Paul as we consider his unique relationships with Lydia and the women of Philippi. In the process, the mirror effect of the Bible will work on us, for we will find ourselves in the stories of the lost women of the Bible. The recovery of these women is important not only to us, it holds profound value for the whole church.

WHEN MEN WEEP

The loss of a woman leaves a terrible void. Just ask any man who has lost one. "Her absence is like the sky, spread over everything," moaned a devastated C. S. Lewis when he lost his beloved wife, Joy, to cancer after three incredibly satisfying years of marriage.[3] Puritan pastor Richard Baxter staggered under the "power of a melting grief" at the loss of his wife, Margaret.[4] A "piercingly bleak emptiness" engulfed a sorrowing Sheldon Vanauken when he lost Davy, the love of his life.[5] Keenly aware of their losses, none of these men would be surprised to discover the first man found weeping in the Bible is mourning the loss of a woman. There is pathos between the lines as the aged Abraham weeps over the lifeless body of his soul mate Sarah (Genesis 23:2). In the wake of such profound loss, real men cry.

If a man can weep openly over the loss of one woman, the whole church has reason to weep the loss of the women of the Bible. Their stories have been buried under layers of low expectations and the belief that God is doing his most important work through men. It is a profound loss—not just to Christian women, but also to Christian men, as we shall see. No doubt these losses can all be traced to the woman who got lost on the opening pages of the Bible. Eve's name tops the list of lost women we need to recover. When Eve got lost, every one of her daughters was affected. Who are we? What is God's calling on our lives? By finding Eve, we will discover the key to unlock the stories of other women in Scripture and the answers to the questions that trouble us. And so we begin our recovery efforts with Eve.

FOCUS: When our lives turn out differently than we expect, when we believe we've missed our true calling as women or that our contributions aren't important, it's easy to get lost. The questions that trouble us when we're lost in our own lives take us deeper in our relationship with God.

FOR DISCUSSION, READ: Psalm 13

1. Describe a situation where you felt lost in your own life or in your relationship with God. *when Ray was so sick & taken to springs (2)*

2. What questions did your struggle raise about yourself? *am I going to be ok*

3. What questions did your struggle raise about God? *Is he going to take Ray*

4. According to Psalm 13, why did King David feel lost in his relationship with God? *he felt God had turned his back on him David*

5. How do your questions compare with the questions he was asking? *Did I have faith in God*

6. Why are we sometimes reluctant to ask these kinds of questions? Why are they important tools to help us grow in our relationship with God? *Pride, shame — yes*

7. What did David expect to discover as he asked his questions of God?

8. Why are the women in the Bible a logical place for us to begin searching for answers? *To know we are not alone*

A Forgotten Legacy—

Eve

She lost the woman God created her to be.

The last time I saw my grandmother, she was a thin shadow of her former self. My daughter was only a few months old, and more than anything I wanted my grandmother to see and hold her great-granddaughter before time ran out on us. I got my wish one afternoon during a visit to the Northwest when my mother drove us to the nursing home. I didn't allow myself to dwell on the fact that neither my grandmother nor Allison would remember this historic meeting that meant so much to me, but the moment I saw my grandmother's blank gaze and sagging form, there was no denying it. The fun-loving, intelligent, energetic woman I had known and admired all my life was nowhere to be seen. In her place a feeble, worn-out body slouched in a wheelchair alongside several other wheelchair-bound individuals in varying stages of decline. It broke my heart to see her so altered. Yet even in her frail and failing condition, the presence of a baby energized her and brought a glimmer (just the slightest) of the woman I remembered. "It's a baby! It's a baby!" she cried in a weak raspy voice as she extended her trembling hands. "Bring him here. We'll take care of him."

Anyone who tried to reconstruct my grandmother from the shell that was left at the last, or who searched for clues to the legacy she passed down to her daughters and granddaughters in this final version of her, would be setting themselves up for failure. The penetrating blue eyes that caused my grandfather's knees to buckle, that devoured countless books including all the classics and just about everything C. S. Lewis ever wrote, that read to her children and made loving books a family tradition were now clouded over by macular degeneration. There was no trace of the beloved teacher of God's Word, who nurtured and influenced so many young women in the faith, not the least of whom were her own two daughters. Her well-worn Bible lay undisturbed on the table beside her bed. The vibrant woman I remembered—the woman God created her to be—was lost somewhere in a fallen, aging body that was no longer hospitable to her marvelous spirit.

The last time anyone saw Eve, she was only a shell of her former self too, a broken-down version of the woman God created her to be. The original Eve was lost in Paradise. Sadly, instead of remembering her in those earlier glory days, the world's memory of her was frozen in time at the worst possible moment—back in the Garden of Eden just as she swallowed a piece of forbidden fruit and served some to her husband. John Milton, the great English poet, couldn't get that image of Eve out of his mind.

> *Her rash hand in evil hour*
> *Forth reaching to the fruit, she pluck'd, she eat:*
> *Earth felt the wound, and Nature from her seat*
> *Sighing through all her works gave signs of woe*
> *That all was lost.*
>
> —JOHN MILTON, *PARADISE LOST*

A bite of fruit, and everyone forgot God's stunning sixth-day assessment: "It is not good for the man to be alone" (Genesis 2:18). We forgot the woman he created as the perfect remedy for man's lack. From the vantage point of hindsight, perhaps the man would have been better off without her, considering the damage she had done. Even Adam seemed to think so when he blamed her for his actions. "The woman you put here with me—she gave me some fruit from the tree, and I ate it" (Genesis 3:12).

Eve's role as instigator in the debacle blotted out the wonder and significance of her creation out of Adam's side, along with Adam's rapturous delight in her. Rarely does anyone recall her as the sole inspiration of the world's first poetry. Even if she lived the rest of her life like Mother Teresa, the world can never forgive what she did to us in Eden. There's no talk of amnesty for the first human being to break rank and rebel against God. No chance we will forget the "rash hand" that reached for the fruit. A few swift movements and it was over. Eve got lost in Paradise—as lost as any woman has ever been. What she was in earlier times is only a dim and distant memory.

THE TROUBLE WITH EVE

We wouldn't dream of doing to my grandmother what we persist in doing to Eve. We forget what Eve was like in her prime and try to reconstruct her legacy from the broken remnants that remained of her at the end. What would be a simple injustice to my grandmother proves far more injurious where Eve is concerned, simply because of her powerful influence over the rest of us, an influence that remains undiminished despite her terrible failure and our attempts to distance ourselves from her. As one writer put it, "There is no way to talk about women without talking about Eve."[1]

God cast the mold for all women when he created Eve. She embodies the secrets of his original blueprint for us. So we rightly turn to her to understand who we are and to discover God's purposes for us. We see and evaluate ourselves, as well as the women in the Bible, through the definition we draw from her. Which makes Eve both powerful and dangerous. Mistakes with regard to our understanding of her are costly for everyone. Like the missile that launches only the slightest fraction off course, we will miss our ultimate target by light-years if we misinterpret Eve. Conversely, a better understanding of Eve as God created her promises much-needed direction and ensures we have a true target in our sights. So before we attempt to understand any other women in the Bible, much less ourselves, we have important groundwork to do with Eve, for she is the foundation of all that follows.

The trouble with Eve is that in the rush to evacuate Eden, we picked up the wrong pieces of her to tell us who we are. On the downside, we're left with the impression of Eve as a temptress, which leads to the belief that women are morally weak and, if given the chance, will bring men down or seize control. This is a *fallen* view of women. On a more positive note, Eve is remembered as wife and mother. Yet even this poses something of a problem. It means little girls must grow up before becoming what God created them to be. Moreover, it excludes women without husbands or children. Eve's old legacy simply doesn't fit us all.

If we want to recover Eve's true legacy, we must begin where the Bible does—with her creation. We must retrace our steps to the Garden of Eden to retrieve the truth God revealed about Eve *before* the serpent showed up. God's definition of the woman and her significant place in his purposes came out in the planning phase of creation when his blueprint for women was spread out on the table in heaven's holy conference room.

EVE'S LOST LEGACY

When Michelangelo painted the magnificent ceiling of the Sistine Chapel in Rome, he painted not one but two frescos of Eve. Next to the ceiling's centerpiece is the fresco that depicts her fall and expulsion with Adam from the Garden of Eden. Theologically, Michelangelo understood Eve's role in what went wrong in Eden. But, in the center of the ceiling—as the focal point of his magnum opus—he pictured God creating Eve out of Adam's side. According to art historians, Michelangelo's artistic decisions were driven by his theology. He somehow wanted to communicate that Eve's creation is central to our understanding of what God intended for us in the first place, what we lost in the Fall, and what Jesus came to restore. Michelangelo's masterpiece gives the full story, including the Fall, but begs the eye to focus on the newly created Eve. Here, at the consummation of creation, God reveals his true vision for humanity and Eve's lost legacy for women. I think the old Italian master was onto something.

In many ways, Eve's creation fulfills the fantasies of a lot of adults who, having suffered through the growing pains and regrets of youth, can only dream of a life that skips the awkward, stubborn, bumpy, learn-the-hard-way stages and starts out as an adult. Wouldn't it be nice to begin life appreciating the value of relationships, education, and opportunities and making the most of them? Eve had that chance. She didn't have to learn to walk, talk, or feed herself (at least we don't think she did). She could easily have started out pondering the big questions of life: "Who am I?" "Where did I come from?" "Why am I here?" If she did, Adam was right there, recovering from surgery, to help her find the answers.

Eve's forgotten legacy resides in explicit statements God made when he created her. First, God created Eve to be *his image bearer*—"in his image and likeness"—and second, to be the *ezer*, or the strong helper. Furthermore, she shared with Adam what theologians call the "Cultural Mandate"—God's command to be fruitful and multiply, to rule and subdue the earth. This global mandate included the call to reproduce physically and to engage in scientific, technological, and artistic pursuits. More importantly, the mandate was also profoundly spiritual and theological—the call to reproduce spiritually by multiplying *worshipers* of the living God and to extend God's gracious rule over every inch of this planet. This staggering enterprise encompasses all dimensions of life and has occupied the human race ever since. God's creation design for Eve applies to *every* woman all the time, from the cradle to the grave.

EVE, GOD'S IMAGE BEARER

The Bible's very first statement about Eve is without question the single most important fact we can know about her. "God created [mankind] *in his own image*, in the image of God he created him; *male and female* he created them" (Genesis 1:27, emphasis added). God created Eve to bear his image—to be like him. This is the Bible's starting point for any definition of what it means to be a woman. It is also one of the most staggering statements in the whole Bible, even though it has become so familiar the shock of it has completely worn off.

In Genesis, however, this announcement is understandably surrounded by intense drama. On the sixth day of creation, we are unexpectedly drawn behind the scenes into the secret council of God, where we overhear a conversation among the Father, Son, and Holy Spirit as they draw up plans to create the man and the woman. "Let us make [mankind] in our image, in our likeness, and let them rule over the fish of the sea and the birds of the air, over the livestock, over all the earth, and over all the creatures that move along the ground" (Genesis 1:26). You can actually sense the excitement.

Frankly, it is a letdown to read what most professional theologians have to say about being God's image bearer. They recite laundry lists of attributes God possesses that he implanted in us and that distinguish us from the rest of creation—qualities like reason, morality, love, wisdom, spirituality, capacity for relationship, and on it goes, like a boring Sunday school lecture that never quite reaches us where we live. What theological technicians say about Eve, while true, utterly fails to capture God's glorious vision. Is the essential meaning of the image of God to distinguish us from and set us above plants and household pets? Is this the sum and substance of the *imago Dei*?

King David didn't think so. He offers us much more in our quest to understand what it means to be made in God's image and he used rather startling language to make his point—so startling some translators have understandably been hesitant to give us the straight translation: "Yet you have made them a little lower than God [Elohim], and crowned them with glory and honor" (Psalm 8:5 NRSV). What does he mean by "a little lower than God"? I would argue that David has in view the rank God bestowed on humans at creation. God is the king, but he called Eve (along with Adam) to be his vice regents—next in rank to God himself in the creation. As his vice regent, as his image bearer, Eve's goal was to align herself with God at every possible level—to share his heart, imitate his ways, love what he loved, and join him in his work. It is the rarest of privileges, the highest of honors, the most daunting challenge imaginable. A simple list of attributes barely scratches the surface of all it means to bear God's image.

Being an image bearer was not a *fait accompli*. Neither Adam nor Eve was a full-fledged image bearer even before they sinned. Rather, it is as though God entrusted to Adam and Eve starter equipment, like the gear the army issues each new recruit. Everyone gets the same equipment. It's what we do with it that makes the difference. Yes, every human is created in God's image with basic qualities and responsibilities we inherit from God. That fact alone invests each person with dignity, worth, and purpose. But those who "walk with God"—who get to know him, follow and imitate his ways—will make much of this high calling. When Eve arrived on the scene, the bar had been raised exceedingly high, for God called her to be like him. "The image of God is ... what we are enroute to becoming"[2]—a calling that invokes us to aspire to be more.

CREATED TO KNOW GOD

Before moving to England, our family often talked playfully about how much fun it would be to meet the queen. Our photo album contains photos of our three-year-old Allison practicing her curtsy "just in case" the queen came to call. She never did. We lived there four years, and not once did she drop by. Not once did the phone ring with an invitation from Buckingham Palace to join Queen Elizabeth for tea. The explanation was simple. She wasn't interested. Didn't even know we existed.

Things have never worked that way with God. From the dawn of creation, he refused to cordon himself off in a palace behind iron gates that admitted only dignitaries and blue bloods with the proper pedigree. By creating us to be his image bearers, he opened himself up to a relationship with us that otherwise would have been hopelessly out of reach.

The call to bear God's image is an invitation to get to know God deeply. On the outskirts of human history—even before a single human set foot on this planet—God opened the door for us to enjoy an intimate relationship with him. The call to bear God's image was intended to whet Eve's hunger to learn all she could about him. It wasn't good enough for Adam to know God and tell her what he was like. Eve needed to know God for herself. In other words, God was calling Eve to be a theologian.

The word *theologian* doesn't appear in the Bible. Old Testament writers used a warmer, user-friendly expression, describing people who "walked with God." A theologian takes a long walk through life with God—living in *his* presence, going *his* way, learning to see the world through *his* eyes, and getting to know *his* character so that trusting him in the dark stretches won't be quite so hard. The theologian sees God at the center of everything. She lives with a profound confidence that he holds the whole world (including her) in his hands. Eugene Peterson described it like this: "If we live by mere happenstance—looking at what is biggest, listening to what is loudest, doing what is easiest—we will live as if God were confined to the margins of our lives. But God is not marginal; God is foundational and central. The person who lives as if God sits on a bench at the edges of life, waiting to be called on in emergencies, is out of touch with reality and so lives badly."[3]

Eve was created to know and walk with God and to make him known to others by reflecting his character in her life. This is a woman's true path to fulfillment and meaning—the only way we will ever discover who we are and find our purpose. And it is accessible to all of us.

But Eve was also called to walk with Adam. Relationship reaches perfection within the holy fellowship of Father, Son, and Holy Spirit. God's image bearers enter into strong relationships with one another. Which brings us to the second part of Eve's lost legacy—her calling as the *ezer*.

march 11, 07

+ mrs Noah

EVE, THE *EZER*

Throughout history the church has always zeroed in on *"ezer"* (pronounced āzer with a long sounding ā, as in razor) as the pre-Fall piece of Eve that defines a woman's role and remained intact despite her sin. God said, "It is not good for the man to be alone. I will make a helper [*ezer*] suitable for him" (Genesis 2:18). The meaning of *ezer*, however, was diminished when translators rendered it "helpmeet" and restricted it to marriage.[4] A woman's mission centered on home and family—vital spheres of ministry to be sure, but only a slice of the vast mission God originally cast by calling women to rule and subdue the earth.

Thinking regarding the *ezer* began to change when scholars pointed out that the word *ezer* is used most often (sixteen of twenty-one occurrences) in the Old Testament to refer to God[5] as Israel's helper in times of trouble. That's when *ezer* was upgraded to *"strong* helper," leaving Christians debating among themselves over the meaning of "strong" and whether this affects a woman's rank with respect to the man. Further research indicates *ezer* is a powerful Hebrew military word whose significance we have barely begun to unpack.[6] The *ezer* is a warrior, and this has far-reaching implications for women, not only in marriage, but in *every* relationship, season, and walk of life.

Earth has always been a war zone. Even before people inhabited the world, the Enemy was on the move. So it makes perfect sense that God used military language to mobilize Eve into action. God created Eve with a mission. The man was alone in the world—the only one on earth who walked by faith. God was preparing to launch the most ambitious enterprise imaginable. The potential for overload, burnout, discouragement, and unbelief was enormous, worse considering the fierce opposition the Enemy was about to mount. Adam couldn't fight these battles alone. So God created the *ezer* as the man's staunchest ally in the life of faith and in fulfilling the Cultural Mandate. Together they exercised dominion and labored to advance God's kingdom in their own hearts and on earth.

Further evidence of the strength and significance of the word *ezer* appeared when men in the Old Testament used *ezer* in naming their sons. Moses named his son Eli-*ezer* (the same name as Abraham's servant), explaining, "My father's God was my helper; he saved me from the sword of Pharaoh" (Exodus 18:4; see Genesis 15:2). First Chronicles 4:4 lists a man named *Ezer*, a descendant of Judah. Abi-*ezer* (my father is help) was among David's mighty warriors (1 Chronicles 11:28). There is wonderful irony in the fact that during New Testament times, one of Jesus' contemporaries, a man outspoken in his belief in women's inferiority to men, was Rabbi Eli-*ezer*.[7] His very name declares the strength of women. (Who says God doesn't have a sense of humor?)

Eve and all her daughters are *ezers*—strong warriors who stand alongside their brothers in the battle for God's kingdom. We do not have to wait until we're grown to become *ezers*. The doctor who announces the birth of a girl might just as well exclaim, "It's an *ezer*!" for we are *ezers* from birth. Marriage is one major arena where the *ezer* stands with the man in battle. It by no means exhausts the possibilities. If the call to rule and subdue the whole earth means anything, God calls the *ezer* to join the man in every sphere of life. Wherever the battle rages for God's kingdom, whenever someone needs a friend, God summons the *ezer* into action. Eve's calling as *ezer* takes us straight into the headwinds of our relationships with men—the most fascinating and at the same time most distressing and dysfunctional aspect of our lives. The paradigm we inherited from Eve is incomplete, however, if we don't grasp her legacy for us at this level.

THE BLESSED ALLIANCE

Sadly, in our world, relationships between men and women have deteriorated so that we jokingly refer to the "Battle of the Sexes," sometimes with a private sense of despair that we'll ever resolve the tensions between us or overcome the difficulties of working together. Yet it was not so in the beginning.

At the dawning of creation, when God had a big job to do (and this was the biggest job ever), the team he put together was male and female. The man and the woman were God's A-Team—his first string of all-stars called to fulfill his ambitious mandate. According to the biblical record, the history of men and women working together is *longer* than men working with men or women working with women. This has profound implications for husbands and wives, but goes well beyond marriage to encompass *every* relationship between men and women in the family, the church, the workplace, and the wider world community. The clear message of the Bible is that God intended for men and women to work together. God put an exclamation point beside his choice of male and female. He *blessed* them before presenting them with their global mandate (Genesis 1:28). They are a *Blessed Alliance*.

God was forging a powerful union between the man and the woman that was essential for the challenges they faced together.

Eve brought to this alliance everything God called her to be as image bearer and *ezer*. God's plan to reveal his image through humanity involved *both* male and female. Nowhere does God's image shine more brightly than when men and women join in serving him together. This vital interaction between men and women enriches every aspect of life. Adam *needed* Eve's gifts and strengths to fulfill his calling, and she needed his gifts too. She was called to enter his struggles, to bolster his faith and obedience to God. The immense calling they shared demanded everything they had to offer and more. Each was called to promote the faithfulness of the other and to get in the way if ever their companion contemplated disobedience.

Every woman's life changes with seasons and circumstances. But for all of us, two callings never change—we are God's image bearers and we are *ezers*. These callings line up perfectly with the two greatest commandments. As image bearer, a woman's chief purpose in life is to love the Lord her God with her whole heart, soul, mind, and strength (Deuteronomy 6:5; Matthew 22:37; Mark 12:30; Luke 10:27). As the *ezer*, her purpose is to love her neighbor as herself, beginning with her husband (her closest neighbor), but encompassing every person she encounters (Leviticus 19:18). The two commands are inseparable. By loving God first and most of all, we learn how to love others as he loves us. If Adam ever usurped God's place in Eve's heart, her love for Adam would degenerate into a destructive force, which is, as we all know, ultimately what happened. So where do things stand with Eve and her daughters, now that the damage has been done? What was left of Eve and her legacy for us, after Paradise was lost?

GETTING LOST

The conversation between Eve and the serpent has drawn enormous attention over the years.[8] It's hard to imagine a more important exchange, given the devastating outcome. What interests me for our purposes, however, is how Eve's callings as image bearer and *ezer* came into play. The serpent's tactics were unnerving. He broached the subject in the most mocking, incredulous manner, making God's command sound rather silly. "Can it really be true—what I've heard—that God said, 'You must not eat from any tree in the garden'?"

You can almost feel Eve stiffen defensively, like a kid being taunted for having an earlier curfew than her peers. She came back with the right answer—sort of. All the trees were accessible, except one. On pain of death, they weren't even to touch that one, which, although not part of God's original command, was actually a good idea. Getting nowhere with this line of argument, the serpent countered by undermining her confidence in God, planting suspicion that God didn't have their best interests at heart and was withholding something good.

It's important to note that Eve's failure wasn't in questioning God's goodness. The Bible is full of similar questions from people earnestly trying to understand God within the appalling realities of a fallen world. Questions actually play a vital role in helping us grow in our relationship with God. They force us to be honest with him and help us probe more deeply into his heart. Asking questions of God was not the problem. The trouble started when neither Eve nor Adam (who was present during the whole discussion)[9] spoke the truth. Despite overwhelming evidence of God's goodness from all that surrounded them, no one spoke up for God.

Nor was Eve out of line to speak or act when she faced the Enemy. The image bearer/strong helper was supposed to join the battle. Before God, she was responsible to think, decide, and act in ways that honored God. Nor was she wrong to initiate. She was called to help Adam, not to create more work for him. It seems to me that, far from trying to overthrow her husband, Eve was actually seeking to benefit him—something any good *ezer* would do.

The real problem was in rejecting and disobeying God's Word. If she had rejected the serpent's proposal and held her ground, no one would ever question her conduct. But instead of relying on the truth, she gave way. God's voice became one of many instead of the one voice against whom all others should be measured. She was completely taken in, tempted, and seduced by the serpent's words. Adam, on the other hand, was *not* seduced or overpowered by seductive charms, as many allege. He ate the fruit knowing full well the serpent's words were false.[10]

I've often puzzled over why Satan's temptation was so overpowering. Why couldn't Eve be content with the abundant variety of other fruit? It almost seems childish to be unable to resist one piece of fruit among so many delicious options. That was before it dawned on me what the serpent was actually offering. The Enemy shrewdly chose the perfect bait, targeting Eve's calling as image bearer. Here was the Alice in Wonderland approach to fulfilling Eve's God-given calling in life. Just sink your teeth into this piece of fruit and presto, "you'll be like God."

One writer, critical of Eve for overstepping her bounds as a woman, suggested things would have turned out better if Eve had insisted, "Let me not be like God. Let me be what I was made to be—let me be a woman."[11] But being like God *was* Eve's true calling as a woman. This was God's design for her. The passion of her heart was to be like God. The serpent couldn't possibly have offered her anything more desirable.

It is sobering to realize that God, not the woman, was the first person to be marginalized on earth. *God* was slighted. Not the man. Eve and Adam turned their backs on God by choosing to become like God *without him*—without walking the long road of faith and obedience and doing the hard work of forging a relationship with him. It was a shortcut that could never deliver what the serpent promised.

Their actions did deliver what God promised. Death. The freedom and joy they once relished just vanished. Their hearts turned cold toward God. Naked and filled with shame, they frantically stitched leaves together to cover themselves. Flimsy fig-leaf coverings were not enough, so they hid themselves instead of stepping out to walk with God in the cool of the evening. Their longings for fellowship with God were displaced by an overwhelming desire to get away. Instead of repentance and sorrow, there was blame. Adam blamed Eve. Eve blamed the serpent. The whole scene was sickening. They were clueless about what they had done and what they were losing. Tragically, in the familiar surroundings of the beautiful Garden that was home, they were lost. Death was in the air, and their losses were incalculable.

ON THE OUTSIDE OF EDEN

So what was it like, the morning after the great crash? After living in the Garden, in harmony with Adam, after enjoying open access to God, what was it like to awaken that first morning in the wilderness knowing they could never go back there again? How very different this was from the first time Eve opened her eyes and heard the jubilant man waxing eloquent over her. No one was reciting poetry now. Tension and distance had come between them. How long would it be before Adam's anger subsided — the anger that pointed the finger of blame at Eve?

Oh, the things we would all take back, if given the chance. Hasty decisions, rash words, and reckless actions that backfired, leaving wounds, closed doors, and estrangements we can't seem to repair. Did Eve relive again and again that fateful moment when she bought the lie and bit into the fruit? Was she depressed over losing Eden and about the rift that had invaded her marriage? Were any tears shed over the loss of God? We only know that her world, her life, her body, her marriage, her work, her relationship with God — all changed forever.

Life in a fallen world was nothing like life in the Garden she once called home. Efforts to subdue and rule the earth now met with resistance as the earth, originally designed for their comfort and safe habitation, turned hostile. Work that once promised satisfaction and joy now required "painful toil."

She and Adam brought suffering on their children too. Death posed a constant threat to their attempts to be fruitful and multiply. The grave has an appetite that never says, "Enough!"[12] The pain of childbirth was not limited to labor pains, as often thought, although labor pain was surely intended. The Hebrew word used for the woman's pain is the same word used for the man's pain in his work. It is *not* the usual Hebrew word for the pangs of childbirth.[13] The pain of bearing children extends far beyond the pain of physical birth. Now, instead of being the joyous, purely hopeful event it should have been, the birth of a child became a source of unavoidable pain for everyone. The child suffers from the brokenness of a fallen world, but also adds to the suffering because of personal fallenness. A child's parents suffer as well because of their helplessness to shield their child from heartache and their inability to change a heart.

Eve cried out in physical pain countless times as she gave birth. That pain was nothing compared to the pain she felt when her firstborn, Cain, murdered her second son, Abel. Pain spread over the planet as the descendants of Adam and Eve lived out their fallenness in relationships with others. The multiplication of true image bearers was now obstructed by spiritual death—the deadness of their children's hearts toward God—for Adam and Eve would multiply after their own kind.

After Eve and Adam ate the forbidden fruit, relationships between men and women collapsed from unity into tension and conflict. Instead of being valued as the man's strongest ally and spiritual resource, the *ezer* became an object to possess and control. The noble calling to rule and subdue the earth in God's name was perverted, as male and female tried to rule and subdue each other. The vast shared global vision God gave them at creation constricted into narrowly defined roles, and male and female divided life into separate spheres. The Blessed Alliance was breaking up.

FOUND AGAIN

God never abandoned his original blueprint. He never threw out his plan for male and female to bear his image, he refused to retire the *ezer*, and he maintained his vision of the Blessed Alliance. God set his jaw with determination when things were at their worst—Paradise was in shambles and a fig-leafed Adam and Eve were standing there making excuses. God's love never stops. His purposes never change. Adam and Eve and their offspring might turn their backs on God. He never turned his back on them or us.

Included in God's shattering words of curse was an unsolicited promise of hope. God promised a redeemer—a descendant of the woman—to engage the serpent in mortal combat and emerge the victor (Genesis 3:15). Amid the shards of the Fall, God picked up the warrior piece of Eve and promised the birth of another much greater warrior. The seed of the woman—Jesus—became humanity's hope, the seed of promise.

Ezers are alive and well throughout biblical history. They come alongside the men in their lives—husband, father, brothers, friends, and colleagues—joining hands to reflect God's image and build his kingdom. The Bible records some glowing moments (along with serious failures) for the Blessed Alliance. At times God orchestrates situations, leaving men no choice but to rely upon the courage and godly resourcefulness of women. Jesus took the Blessed Alliance to new heights by joining men and women in one body—his church. Although male-female relationships remain a place of struggle, occasionally, even today, we catch glimpses of what God intended.

The Blessed Alliance came to life when a board of hardworking deacons invited a woman in the church to attend one of their meetings to discuss ministry opportunities in their church. In reality, they were "including" her as a friendly gesture toward the women in the church, counting on her to recruit other female volunteers to work. What they discovered in their interactions with her was something they didn't expect. They actually needed her to help them minister more effectively as deacons. Her insights into the people who needed their care revealed dimensions of ministry they had overlooked and opened ways to minister more compassionately. Instead of doing *her* a favor by giving her a place at the table, her influence and wisdom enhanced *their* ministries. It was another gentle reminder of God's assessment in the beginning, "It is not good for the man to be alone."

Although it has been years since my grandmother shed her frail body and entered the arms of Jesus, the woman I knew and loved in her younger days lives on in my memory and continues to inspire me. Eve's glorious legacy lives on today too. She gives all women more to live for. We are God's image bearers. There is no higher calling. We are *ezers*—chosen by God to soldier alongside our brothers as a Blessed Alliance, advancing Christ's kingdom in the hearts of people all around us.

Eve's threefold legacy—that we are God's image bearers, *ezer*-warriors, and members of the Blessed Alliance—provides a clear lens through which we will examine the women in Scripture and gain a fresh vision for ourselves. In the chapters that follow, we will look at each woman's story to see how she lived up to this rich legacy that all women inherit from Eve.

The woman we turn to next is a perfect first candidate for us to try out this forgotten legacy for women. Mrs. Noah was so lost, she doesn't even make the long list of women in the Bible. But she is on our short list and has a powerful message for us.

FOCUS: Eve has enormous influence over women's lives today because she was the first woman God created. We want to recover Eve's forgotten legacy and rediscover God's creation blueprint for women.

EVE'S STORY: Genesis 1:26–31; 2:18–25; 3:1–24; 4:1–2

FOR DISCUSSION, READ: Genesis 1:26–31; 2:18–25

1. Prior to reading this chapter, how have you understood God's calling for you as a woman, based on the story of Eve? Where do you expect to find your greatest fulfillment in life?

2. What kinds of women or stages of a woman's life are left out of your definition of a woman's calling? Does your definition ever leave *you* out?

3. What is the Bible's first statement about women and why is this the highest possible calling for any human being?

4. Why is *image bearer* both a description of who we are as human beings and a vision of what God created us to become?

5. What does it mean to be an *ezer*? How does it affect your view of yourself to realize the *ezer* is a warrior?

6. How does being an *ezer* affect our relationships with those around us? How are we *ezers* for our friends and loved ones?

7. Describe some examples you have seen of the Blessed Alliance or where you have seen it lacking.

8. How do our callings as image bearers, *ezers*, and members of the Blessed Alliance reinforce our need to know God better?

THE UNKNOWN SOLDIER —

Mrs. Noah

A woman can really get lost even in a good marriage.

A military wife learned a lot about herself during the height of the Vietnam War when for months her husband was in active combat overseas and she remained back home in sole command of their little family. Her husband's absence and constant peril pushed her out into unfamiliar territory, where she was forced to summon from within strengths and abilities she never knew existed. These gifts were indispensable now that she was carrying the full responsibility for their children and for herself, as well as guarding her husband's morale. From time to time (whenever she could stop to catch her breath), she thought about how much better the early years of their marriage might have been if she had awakened sooner to how much more she had to offer. She looked ahead and wondered if their marriage would grow stronger when her husband returned home. Would he have a new appreciation and respect for the gifts and strengths God gave her, or would she, like so many other women, be honorably discharged and returned to earlier peacetime dependencies?

Mrs. Noah got lost in her marriage. Among the lost women of the Bible, she has all but vanished from sight. Her story (which may have been a good one) died with her and remains buried to this day because the story that got told was her husband's. She was one of eight individuals to survive the world's worst natural disaster, yet every so-called "complete" list of women in the Bible leaves her out. Even feminist commentaries, determined to highlight every mention of women in the Bible, skip right past her as though she never existed.

This oversight isn't because she didn't have a story to tell. If she were alive today, she'd find the media camped out all over her front lawn and the phone ringing incessantly with Barbara Walters angling for one of her revealing interviews. Knowing how gripped we all were by the stories told by ordinary people who survived 9/11 or the Asian tsunami disaster of 2004, you can be sure Mrs. Noah's story would grab the headlines. In the biblical record, however, she fades into anonymity, lost in the shadow of her more illustrious husband. Despite her historic ordeal, we know next to nothing about her. We don't even know her name.

This lack of information worried my scholarly husband when I casually mentioned my plan to devote a whole chapter to Noah's wife. He feared I might be heading off into the murky waters of speculation. I assured him there was plenty to say about her without a bit of speculation. Turns out I was right.

In an odd way, Mrs. Noah is ideal for our discussion of lost women *precisely because* we know so little about her. She helps us see there are no exceptions to Eve's legacy for women. Eve's legacy—that God created women to be his image bearers, *ezers*, and vital members of the Blessed Alliance—is universal, encompassing every woman's life, no matter how obscure, insignificant, or forgotten we think we are. God's purposes aren't just for those who stand in the spotlight. They apply equally to those of us who remain hidden in the shadows.

Talking about Mrs. Noah is a little like wandering through a cemetery and stopping at a headstone that bears the name and dates of a woman we never knew. Perhaps from the headstone nearest hers we can safely deduce she was a wife. There might even be other headstones in the vicinity that appear to be those of her children. From her dates, we may figure out that she lived through an era of great adversity—the Great Depression, for example, or the Civil War. From dates on her husband's headstone, we can tell she was a widow. Dates on other headstones might lead to an educated guess that this unknown woman once wept near where we are standing, over a beloved child who preceded her in death. Beyond these sketchy bits of information, we are left completely in the dark concerning other details of her life. Her full story remains a mystery, unknown and unknowable to us, buried with her body underneath the grass. Still, the lack of information doesn't prevent us from wondering. After our discussion about Eve, we actually have some rather pointed questions for the woman lying beneath the headstone—and for the senior matron emerging from the ark with the legendary Noah.

LEARNING FROM MRS. NOAH

Mrs. Noah's life is a blank slate on which to write the generic questions that Eve's story generates, questions we regularly need to be asking of the women in the Bible and, more particularly, of ourselves. Where does she fit into God's purposes in her specific time and place? How did she contribute to God's kingdom? How did being God's image bearer change her outlook on life? What battles was this *ezer* called to fight? What was her theology and how did it help her survive? How does the Blessed Alliance show up in her story? In other words, who were the men in her story and did she align with them to serve God?

The unknown Mrs. Noah gives us a practice run at examining a real woman's life through the lens of Eve's legacy without being prejudiced or distracted by prior knowledge of her successes or her failures. She teaches us how to think about ourselves. By piecing together enough sketchy details to reconstruct the basic contours of her life, we can begin to see how the issues facing Mrs. Noah relate to our own lives in all their rich diversity. (Feel free to substitute another family member, friend, or coworker in place of Noah and to use other venues for the ark—a corporate office, an academic classroom, a ministry, or a van full of kids—wherever God has placed you.) Through Mrs. Noah's example we can find freedom and courage to live more faithfully for Christ in every possible circumstance, whether we're married or alone, eight or eighty-eight, out in front or in the background.

THE SEARCH FOR MRS. NOAH

If it has happened once, it has happened dozens of times. I am often introduced at conferences by a wife who is married to one of my husband's former students. Typically the introduction goes something like this: "Let me tell you a little about Carolyn," then promptly shifts to, "Her husband, Frank, is a seminary president and professor of historical theology ..." followed by a lengthy description of my husband's degrees, accomplishments, and his impact on her husband's life. Somehow I get lost in my own introduction.

Mrs. Noah's introduction sounds a lot like that. Her husband, Noah, was a giant of faith. He stood alone when the rest of the world turned its back on God, and God singled him out for a daunting assignment that secured his place in the Bible as well as in history. His epic story is so well known, little children can tell you all about it in minute detail. They might mention "Noah's wife" in passing. But they have considerably more to say about Noah. Mrs. Noah can't even compete with the extensive list of animals that children find especially fascinating in the retelling of the story of the great flood.

The wife of a former NFL football player told me she could relate. She recalled many times being shoved aside by eager fans who wanted her husband's autograph. Not only was she unimportant, she was in the way. Another of my friends, after reflecting on how Mrs. Noah was eclipsed by her husband, remarked, "We all know how that feels."

The Bible devotes five whole chapters (Genesis 6–10) to Noah's story and mentions him again with well-deserved honor in Chronicles, the Prophets, the Gospels, and the Epistles. In contrast, Mrs. Noah barely reaches the level of a footnote. Genesis acknowledges her existence five times, never once by name, and never for anything she does or for any quality or contribution that distinguishes her from anyone else. Not everyone accepts the fact that so little is known about her. When *USA Today* conducted a survey of biblical knowledge, they included the question: "Who was Noah's wife?" Forty percent of those responding believed her name was "Joan of Ark." So what do we know about Mrs. Noah?

FRAGMENTS OF A LIFE

The first fragment of her life is that Mrs. Noah lived during terrible times. *Wickedness* and *violence* weren't news bites about trouble happening a safe distance from "respectable" neighborhoods. The whole culture was infected. God's "heart was filled with pain" (Genesis 6:6). He grieved because wickedness was rampant among the people and "every inclination" of their hearts was "only evil all the time" (Genesis 6:5). The whole world was in crisis.

Mrs. Noah could sympathize with women who live in fear of drive-by shootings. Living in a society of violence, she was no stranger to the kinds of anxieties mothers feel when sending their children off to school where the first test they must pass each day is a metal detector. Even our post-9/11 jitters would have touched a nerve with her. She lived in a violent culture that made no room for God. The consequences were alarming. It was a distressing and dangerous time to be alive.

But the danger from a violent neighbor or passerby was nothing compared to the threat that hung overhead. I remember the uneasiness we felt in Oregon back in 1980 as we monitored the growing bulge on Mount St. Helens from the increasing pressure of gases and fumes within. For weeks we knew the volcano was going to blow. We just didn't know exactly when. People at the base of the mountain fled their homes with whatever they could cart away. That's what people do when they realize their lives are in peril.

In Mrs. Noah's day, people weren't the least concerned about impending disaster. No one cared about God or how he viewed the way they were living. No one feared his judgment. No one had ever witnessed the terrifying power of water, so far as we know, or even felt a drop of rain.[2] So Noah's warnings sounded like a bunch of silly nonsense. "Wild-eyed old man!" People simply laughed and shook their heads. These were the difficult days of Mrs. Noah.

The second fragment we know about Mrs. Noah is the fact that she was married. Her identity and her claim to fame are bound up in the single fact that she was "Noah's wife." The Bible doesn't tell us whether she shared her husband's unflinching faith in God or not. What we *can* say is that her marriage assignment was a tough one. Her husband was one of a kind—"a righteous man, blameless among the people of his time, and he walked with God" (Genesis 6:9). Noah is a bright spot in the early history of the world. This man stood out from the rest of the population because of his faithful devotion to God. It is, however, a mixed blessing to be married to such a man. Strong godly character, while incredible in a husband, comes at a stiff price in a world that rejects his values. The size of the ark alone, not to mention his preaching, exposed Noah to the ridicule and smirks of neighbors. Any preacher's wife can tell you, it is painful to see your husband mocked and rejected. It is lonely and isolating when God sets you apart from everyone else.

By modern Christian ministry standards, Noah was an utter disaster. After years of impassioned evangelism, he didn't add a single name to the ark's passenger list. Not many pastors today could survive an annual report like that. Fruitlessness is a heavy burden to bear if you're the preacher. Noah must have had his low moments. We don't talk much about that part of the ark builder's story.

Clearly, the Bible doesn't measure a person by the same standards we use today, even in the church. Generations later, Noah's epitaph read: "By faith Noah, when warned about things not yet seen, in holy fear built an ark to save his family. By his faith he condemned the world and became heir of the righteousness that comes by faith" (Hebrews 11:7). He was a bold and courageous man of faith, who followed God no matter how ridiculous he looked or what it cost him personally. Neither he nor his wife could see the future to know how history would vindicate him. Instead of enjoying that sweet consolation, they lived with the undeniable and disheartening reality that Noah's ministry was a failure.

A third fact we know is that Mrs. Noah was a mother of the first rank. We don't need to know a thing about her parenting skills to know she earned high marks as a mother in the ancient culture. In ancient times, as in some Third World countries today, the culture gauged a woman's success and value by the number of sons she bore her husband. Her reproductive successes determined her husband's stature in the community, not to mention his survival. More sons translated into greater economic strength and political power for a man. They also perpetuated his name and estate for another generation. Marriage without sons was a disaster and usually prompted such radical measures as polygamy. In future chapters, we will see the heart-wrenching anguish this common standard of measurement produced in the lives of women who were infertile. But in Mrs. Noah's case, the standard worked in her favor. She earned top ratings for having delivered three sons—Shem, Ham, and Japheth—to carry on their father's name. Her three sons grew up and joined their father in building the ark. As a woman, Mrs. Noah could hold her head up high in the community. She had done her duty, and done it well.

Fourth, Mrs. Noah was a survivor. No other flood, earthquake, hurricane, or war in history caused the loss of life and destruction of property left behind by this global flood. Footage of regional floods over the past few decades shows appalling devastation and certainly exposes how we've sugarcoated the catastrophe Noah and his family endured. Our children's books picture a bright-eyed Noah and company emerging from a cozy ark into a rainbow-encircled paradise, when in fact the graphic post-flood scenes were anything but suitable material for children's storybooks.

The flood brought deep personal losses for our heroine. The waters that covered the earth swept away the only world she had ever known—the life she and Noah worked so hard to build. Friends, relatives, her home, her community, and her way of life were gone. Everything was lost. Like the *Titanic* in reverse, the whole world sank beneath the waves, and only the enormous vessel remained afloat. It's hard to imagine going through a catastrophe like that without battling depression. If Mrs. Noah wasn't an animal lover, she had a whole new dimension of trauma during her confinement in the ark. And when the pounding rains subsided and the waters finally receded, she faced the daunting prospect of starting over from scratch in her old age.

Finally, she was a daughter of Eve—the torchbearer of Eve's bright legacy for future generations of women. In a way, she was something of a second Eve, for every woman born after the flood descended from Mrs. Noah. She had a lot to pass on, for she was God's image bearer and an *ezer*. With her husband, she shared the same call to know and walk with God in a dark and evil age. This was her high calling as a woman. As a daughter of Eve, she bore heavy responsibility to be fruitful and multiply worshipers of the living God and to rule and subdue the earth under his gracious and holy reign. And Mrs. Noah, along with her husband, was a crucial member of the Blessed Alliance. So how does Eve's legacy fit into the life of Mrs. Noah? Did her own walk with God brace her soul to face the losses of the past and to tackle the enormous task of rebuilding that lay ahead?

THE QUESTIONS WE SHOULD ASK

From these few fragments of her life we can already see we have a lot in common with Mrs. Noah. In our world, as in hers, there are days when it feels like more is sinking than is staying afloat. And her story, no matter how heroic and newsworthy it may have been, didn't get written up. Most of our stories won't either. Eve's glorious legacy draws the mysterious Mrs. Noah out of the shadows and confronts her with important questions about God's mission for her in the crisis. This time none of the conventional answers will work.

The Bible captures a segment of Mrs. Noah's life that comes after she has already done her wifely duty. Her sons are raised and married. Her busy, overwhelming days of caring for small children are over. As a mother, she has joined the honorable ranks of empty nesters. Ahead lies the happy prospect of grandchildren. Yet, just as she is easing into a life of settled satisfaction, God's earthshaking message to Noah turns Mrs. Noah's world upside down. Was this just between Noah and God? Or is there a place for Mrs. Noah in what God is doing?

In a way, she reminds me of my great-aunt Edith on one of her visits to our family in Portland, Oregon. Aunt Edith had grown elderly and feeble, was quite deaf, and was really more of a hindrance than a help. Having always been an active woman, she could hardly bear to sit and fold her hands while my mother and grandmother prepared the family dinner. She wanted something to do. I remember how everyone scrambled to come up with little tasks to keep her occupied and help her feel useful without risking chipped china or a spoiled recipe.

When it comes right down to it, Mrs. Noah was the one person on board that ark who didn't seem to have an obvious role. The usual ways a woman had of contributing were all behind her. Once the ark door clicked shut behind them, it would be a long time before she set a fine table for her husband or cleaned the house. From the biblical record, it appears her childbearing days were over too, so she was sidelined there as well despite the fact that there was an empty earth to repopulate. That mission fell to her daughters-in-law. We're left with lingering questions. Had her usefulness expired? Was she dead weight on the ark? A luxury passenger? A disinterested spectator? Did others try to think of "little things" for her to do so she wouldn't feel left out?

One of my heroes, an older friend in Canada, put a different slant on this kind of "washed-up" thinking when she made the difficult move from her independent home into an assisted living facility. All her life she had vigorously engaged in ministry—serving for years as a missionary in Cuba before the Communist revolution. Now in her eighties, it looked to her as though her days of fruitful ministry were over. To friends she confided in a letter, "I felt I no longer had a reason for living and that life now had no meaning or purpose."

When she took her despair to God and then looked around her, she was surprised and invigorated by what she saw. He opened her eyes to new opportunities right in front of her, and she willingly embraced her new assignment from God. She was surrounded by people who needed her spiritual ministries—a mission field all her own. The world, and even the church, may retire us from active duty and consider that we've done our part after families are raised or we reach a certain age or state of health. But God never retires his *ezers*. He may change our location and circumstances, but he always has crucial work for us to do.

Mrs. Noah may not have had a traditional role to fulfill. But God's call to Noah gave her a mission too. She was an *ezer*, after all, and Noah needed her help. The whole of humanity had turned away from God, and Noah stood alone because he "walked with God"—the continuous day-by-day relationship with God that distinguishes the child of God from everyone else. To his neighbors Noah was a fool, but in God's eyes he was *righteous* and *blameless*—qualities God's image bearers acquire by a close association with God. After Enoch, Noah is the second person named in the Bible who "walked with God." This implies a depth of intimacy, companionship, and unity that every child of God should seek.

No one knows where Mrs. Noah stood with God, but the question is one she needed to answer. Did she side with her neighbors or with her husband? There was no middle ground. How we wish the Bible made the same strong statements about Mrs. Noah that it does about Noah. But we are left with silence. Still, as God's image bearer, she was called to walk before the face of God as a righteous, blameless woman.

No one knows how Mrs. Noah fared as an *ezer* either. What was Noah's strong helper to do in this situation? Pound nails, herd animals, and swab decks with the men? There's no limit to what an *ezer* will do. After surviving three sequential hurricanes in Florida, I can say on fairly good authority that when you're battening down the hatches for a natural disaster of this magnitude, any physical help that's offered is welcome.

More importantly, Noah needed his wife's spiritual help. Even the greatest of God's servants have their low moments. Noah might put on a brave face in public and maybe even in front of their sons. But at day's end, like most men, he let down his guard at home. A man—even one with Noah's spiritual maturity—has a hard time hiding his discouragement from his wife. If Mrs. Noah's spiritual antennae were tuned to Noah, she sensed his ups and downs. Christian leadership can be a lonely place. Leaders often don't have the freedom to reveal their doubts and struggles to others since everyone relies on them to set a strong example. Noah might be able to maintain a brave face in public. He'd have a harder time concealing those struggles from his wife—nor should he. God called her to come alongside him in his struggles and to share his burdens. A married *ezer* like Mrs. Noah is first in line when it comes to fortifying her husband spiritually.

When Noah fell to his knees, discouraged and helplessly dependent on God, was his wife kneeling at his side? Did she cling to God's character and join her husband in the lonely exhausting battle to trust God as they walked into the great unknown? Was she with him in his struggles, or did she quietly tiptoe away until his mood changed for the better? One thing is clear. If she didn't stand with Noah, his job was considerably more difficult, for he was soldiering alone. If she entered his struggles and got under his burdens with him, then his load was lighter, for the two of them were standing together against the world. If anything, Mrs. Noah had one of the toughest and most important assignments in the whole crisis—to minister encouragement and hope to Noah. But realistically, where does a woman find the resources for such a job, especially when her own world is falling apart and she has her own fears and doubts to think about? Where can she find strength to offer to someone else?

MRS. NOAH'S THEOLOGY

Some years ago, a modern descendant of slaves traced his family roots back to Africa. His trail led to the harbor where captured Africans were loaded as living cargo onto ships. In cramped and incomprehensibly inhumane conditions (which many didn't survive), these prisoners sailed to foreign lands and to a life of slavery, suffering, and hard labor. He walked through the darkened holding cell where his ancestors spent their final hours in Africa and he stood in the passageway where the slave ships once docked.

It had been ages since the last slaves were abducted from their homeland through that opening. So much had changed. Now there were no waiting ships, no repressed sobs, no clinking chains, no shuffle of reluctant feet as slaves filed onto waiting ships. Only the endless sea with the sunlight dancing on the surface and the quiet lapping of the water against the old stone walls. To the uninformed eye, this was just another tranquil seascape. But when the great-grandson of slaves stepped back into the darkness of the holding cell and viewed the sea, framed by the darkened doorposts through which his ancestors passed in unrelieved agony to a future of misery, he described the ocean scene as the "infinity of suffering."

Like the descendant of slaves, Mrs. Noah gazed out on a similar scene. From the safety of the ark, she looked through a window on the vast receding floodwaters and contemplated what lay ahead. To the uninformed eye, it was just another tranquil seascape—endless water with the sunlight dancing on the surface and the quiet lapping of the waves against the sides of the massive ark. But this too was the "infinity of suffering"—the grand stage on which the rest of human history would play out.

The family survived their terrible ordeal, along with all the living creatures inside the ark. But stowed away, safe and sound inside the ark, was another survivor no one had counted on. *Sin* had come through the storm without a scratch. The brave new world the Noah family rebuilt was just as broken as the old one. A second Eden was not to be. Sin was alive and well—still destroying lives and turning hearts away from God. Noah and his wife and their family probably already saw signs of trouble as they waited together for days inside the ark for the land to dry and tried to get along with each other.

We know nothing about Mrs. Noah's theology. We know her husband was a man of God, but the Bible is silent on the subject of what Mrs. Noah knew or believed about God. She certainly didn't draw her theology from the Bible, for during her lifetime, the Bible didn't exist. Knowledge of God passed by word of mouth from one generation to the next—stories of creation and of the Fall—and also from observing God's creation and from his intervention in their lives. Whether she paid attention or not, God was revealing a lot about himself to Mrs. Noah even through the ark itself.

When Mrs. Noah gazed out on the waters, did she dread what lay beyond? The losses? The mess of the aftermath? Did she groan at the thought of starting over again or sink beneath one last wave of depression? Mrs. Noah couldn't open a Bible, join a prayer group, or seek a Christian friend to help see her through this crisis. Those options didn't exist. Her only lifeline was her relationship with God. And God was making himself known to her in powerful ways if she only had eyes to see it. Right in front of her was a powerful message that contained exactly what she needed to carry on with courage, no matter what she faced in the future. As she looked at the endless waters, if she stepped back into the shadows to view the vast sea, framed within the window of the ark, she might have gained a new perspective.

The challenges and losses that awaited her looked different when framed in the window of the ark—an enormous physical reminder of God's character and loyal love for them. The ark itself provided tangible evidence that they were in God's hands and that he is truly good. She could tell herself (and one hopes she did) that the same God who rescued them from destruction and carried them safely through the storm would be with them in the venture ahead. Even the aftermath of a catastrophe looks hopeful when framed in the ark of God's sovereignty, goodness, and love. As Mrs. Noah stepped out of the ark and onto dry land, the rainbow in the sky reinforced this vision of her life. She belonged to God, and she mattered to him.

JOAN OF ARK

So what happens when Johnny comes marching home from Vietnam, Iraq, or some other battlefront in a flurry of yellow ribbons, ticker-tape parades, and medal ceremonies? When this decorated hero meets the press, does anyone notice the other hero in this war—the unknown soldier standing in the shadows who steeled his courage from afar while holding down the battlefront at home? Will Johnny himself notice and realize how much he needs this valiant warrior's contributions for the "peacetime" battlefronts ahead?

One of the post-war traumas faced by military families is the readjustment to civilian life that a husband and wife make once a term of duty is fulfilled or the war is over. The potential for loss is tremendous. It's easy to assume that a wife's gifts of leadership, strength, and wisdom—so essential during the crisis—are suddenly nonessentials now that there's a man at home. If Mrs. Noah was the strong helper God meant for her to be, one wonders if Noah learned through his ordeal how indispensable she was to him, or if, once they set foot on dry land, he embraced the culture's old ways of thinking about her. What does a man stand to lose when his wife's gifts and abilities are tucked away and forgotten until another crisis (or his reassignment) renders them necessary again? You'd think a military man would be the first to see the value of having a seasoned warrior next to him and be quick to encourage (even urge) his wife to cultivate and employ the gifts God entrusted to her because he knows the difference she makes in his life.

The rainbow reminds us of God's promise, that there will never be another worldwide flood. Most wars between nations also come to an eventual end. But the battle for God's kingdom rages on. No army is fit for battle if half the soldiers are disarmed. The Enemy is fierce and will not relent. God calls every soldier—male or female, young or old, married or single—to be battle-ready at all times. The Bible addresses women as warriors in combat—from creation right up to the end of human history. Jesus gave women a solemn stewardship when he entrusted to them gifts for his church. He calls us to serve his purposes in the lives of people all around us.

The Bible draws a curtain across the story of Mrs. Noah. We can only wonder how well or how badly she did and whether she and Noah formed a Blessed Alliance. She leaves us with a lot of unanswered questions. But in a strange way she provides some very important answers.

Mrs. Noah got lost in Noah's shadow, but in God's eyes, she was never lost. Whether a woman is out in front or the unknown soldier hidden in the shadows, whether she's facing a crisis or having an ordinary day, she has a vital role in God's purposes.

Our ministries make a difference in other people's lives. God calls us to share the burdens of others, to come alongside a husband or a friend and aid them in their walk with God. Mrs. Noah puts those options in front of us. We are God's image bearers. We are *ezers*. Retirement isn't an option. Mrs. Noah had a vital place in God's purposes. The world was going down, and she was needed for the battle. Maybe "Joan of Ark" wasn't such a wild guess after all.

The next woman we will consider was never in any danger of getting lost in obscurity. Sarah is one of the most prominent women in the Bible. But when she couldn't fulfill the traditional role her culture spelled out for women and it looked to her like God was squeezing her out of his purposes, she got lost.

FOCUS: The Bible tells us next to nothing about Mrs. Noah, so she provides the perfect test case for us to see how Eve's legacy applies to a real woman's life. By viewing Mrs. Noah as God's image bearer, the *ezer*, and an active member of the Blessed Alliance, we will learn to see ourselves in the same way.

MRS. NOAH'S STORY: Genesis 6:1–9:19

FOR DISCUSSION, READ: Genesis 6:11–22; 7:7–13; 8:14–18

1. Describe a situation where you felt lost in someone else's shadow.

2. How did Mrs. Noah get lost?

3. How did her twin callings as God's image bearer and *ezer* define her mission in the crisis that was unfolding?

4. What opportunities did she and Noah have to forge and serve God as a Blessed Alliance? How could they be stronger together than if they worked alone?

5. Describe the reasons Mrs. Noah had to fear and dread the future.

6. What situation are you facing now that, like Mrs. Noah's uncertain future, fills your heart with fear and dread?

7. What did Mrs. Noah already know about God that offered her hope no matter what lay ahead?

8. What difference does it make to put the frame of God's character around your situation?

LIFE IN THE MARGINS—

Sarah

D*id it ever occur to you that God might not want your life?"*

My brow wrinkled with confusion and consternation when that question was lobbed my way like a hand grenade from someone I thought was a trusted ally. As a matter of fact, she was just trying to jar me by showing where my negative thoughts were leading. I was feeling sorry for myself—comparing God's interest and activity in the lives of others around me with his silence and what I perceived as his disinterest toward me. Everyone else was getting married, starting families, and moving forward with their lives. Nothing seemed to be happening with me. Everywhere I turned I saw signs that my life was at a standstill. Much as I tried to brush it off, the truth hurt. Had God forgotten me? Was I less of a woman because I was single? Was there a place for me in God's purposes if I never married or never had children, or if I did and (God forbid) I lost them?

Of all of the women in this book, Sarah's story highlights the threatening issues inherent in the discussion of God's calling for women and what gives a woman's life meaning and purpose. Perhaps that is why I identify most with Sarah. She got lost in the very place a woman is supposed to find herself. Sarah got lost at home.

I connect with Sarah for lots of reasons. We both grew up with three brothers. I can imagine the two of us having a good, long feisty chat about the woes of being outnumbered and the pros and cons of life with brothers. At another level, I have enormous sympathy for all those times she and Abraham packed up their belongings and moved to a new location. I knew Sarah was a kindred spirit when my intrepid Sunday school teacher produced a map tracing Abraham's endless wanderings. Sarah and Abraham moved so many times, the lines of their migrations looked like someone dropped a plate of spaghetti on the ancient Near East. For the first thirteen years of my marriage, I kept storage boxes and packing containers ready for our next move. Like nomads, we moved from the East Coast to the West Coast, then to England, and finally to Florida, with a lot of little moves at each location. I still have to pinch myself when I realize I've been living in the same house now for over ten years. Sarah and Abraham never found a place to call home. In fact, the only piece of land they ever owned was the plot Abraham bought to bury Sarah.

Sarah's story also calls to mind my family's annual Christmas letter. For as long as I can remember, my parents have sent out a holiday letter updating friends and family. I never gave those letters much thought until after college, when those one or two sentences about me started sounding like summer reruns. My brothers were finishing graduate degrees, launching their careers, getting married, moving to interesting places, and, better yet, adding the names of their newborns. In painful contrast, my life was going nowhere, and it didn't help to see that in print, year after year. I joked about it from time to time, but underneath I felt a sinking feeling that Christmas came to the rest of my family but never to me. Somehow when God was distributing presents, I got lost in the shuffle.

LOST IN A WORLD OF MEN

Sarah makes her first appearance near the end of one of those long genealogies we tend to skip over when we're reading through the Bible (Genesis 11:10–32). The segment that contains her name drops early clues that Sarah was already lost.

With the words "This is the account of Terah," the focus of biblical history narrows to a single family in Ur of the Chaldeans in Mesopotamia, which is somewhere in southern Iraq. From there the narrative fans out in three directions through Terah's sons, Abraham, Nahor, and Haran, and their descendants. This is the genealogy of hope because, through Abraham, God was formally launching his plan of redemption that ultimately led to Christ. The men of the family (Sarah's three brothers) became the pillars of biblical history. These three strong tributaries of Terah's family went their separate ways, but reunited generations later when Abraham's male descendants (Isaac, Jacob, and Boaz) married female descendants of his brothers (Rebekah, Leah, Rachel, and Ruth). If, instead of a genealogy, Terah had composed a holiday letter about his family, you'd think he'd at least have tried to find something positive to say about Sarah, who appears to have been his only daughter—his "princess," or Sarai, as they used to call her. Instead, Sarah got lost.

Sarah's true place in the family wasn't revealed until some twenty-four years down the road when Abraham got into a predicament and told everyone she was his half sister (they had different mothers). In this genealogy, however, she is dropped from her high-ranking position as Terah's daughter and entered in the family register as *Abraham's wife*, implying that her connection to the family was solely by marriage. This reflected the patriarchal culture, where daughters had less value than sons and a woman's identity was tied to her husband. I did not grow up in her culture, but I know I'd feel some sense of loss if my own family started regarding me as an in-law.

Then, in words that would have sent a dagger straight through Sarah's heart, the narrator adds the following note: "Now Sarai was barren; she had no children" (Genesis 11:30). This was the definitive statement about Sarah, exposing an open wound and simultaneously eliminating her from the big things God was doing in her family. As we learned from Mrs. Noah, in the ancient world the value of a woman was measured simply by counting her sons. By this calculation, Sarah scored a zero. Her sole contribution in the most important family in the Bible was to produce a son for her husband, and she didn't have what it took. According to the family record, Sarah had two strikes against her. She was a woman in a man's world, and she was barren. Everyone had a role in God's purposes except Sarah. Already she was sliding toward the margins of the story.

THE SOUND OF SILENCE

Sarah was sixty-five and her husband seventy-five when God first spoke these history-changing words to Abraham: "Leave your country, your people and your father's household and go to the land I will show you. I will make *you* into a great nation and I will bless *you*; I will make *your name* great, and *you* will be a blessing" (Genesis 12:1–2, emphasis added). Abraham was undoubtedly elated by God's call, but his promises posed serious problems for Sarah. He talked about *Abraham's* calling and *Abraham's* future. God hadn't spoken a word about Sarah.

God's silence concerning Sarah must have chilled her to the bone. The nagging uncertainties that run the length of her story first rear their ugly heads here. Was there a place in God's plan for Sarah, or did he care only about Abraham? Was there a blessing for Sarah too?

God's silence is one of the most disconcerting experiences any of his children endure. We can persevere through just about anything so long as we sense the warmth of his presence and the reassuring comfort of his love. But courage melts and we are taken hostage by fear and hopelessness when God seems far away. Those long stretches of unanswered prayer, the problems that only seem to get worse, the sleepless nights and anxious days, the endless waiting for God to show up can drive us to despair. The psalmist knew the agonies of God's silence and spoke for all of us when he lamented, "For if you are silent, I might as well give up and die" (Psalm 28:1 NLT).

Sarah suffered God's stony silence for twenty-four long years after we first meet up with her in Genesis and who knows how many years of waiting and monthly disappointments before that. Silence in response to her tears and pleadings for a child. Silence in the beautiful promises that never included her. Silence that only reinforced Sarah's fears that God remembered Abraham, but had forgotten her.

THE POWER OF FEAR

Abraham had some shining moments. What he did when his safety was threatened wasn't one of them. Twice he moved his family into a danger zone, where he feared the men of the land would kill him to get to his beautiful wife. To save his own skin, Abraham, with little regard for Sarah's safety, instructed her to prove her love for him by telling the half-truth that he was her brother instead of her husband (Genesis 20:13). Twice she complied and put her neck on the block to save his.

Abraham protected himself, but Sarah was abducted first into Pharaoh's harem, and years later King Abimelech of Gerar took her. We don't like to deal with this part of the story, but leading Old Testament experts believe that while Abimelech never touched her, Pharaoh's conduct toward her was anything but innocent. A straightforward reading of the biblical text seems to confirm this. Pharaoh reproached Abraham for deceiving him. "Why did you say, 'She is my sister,' so that *I took her to be my wife*?" (Genesis 12:19, emphasis added). Sexually assaulted or not, Sarah must have been shattered. What kind of husband would do what Abraham did? Twice? What was left of Sarah after even her identity as a wife was taken away?

SARAH FIGHTS BACK

Anyone reading the Bible from a twenty-first-century Western point of view is sure to experience culture shock sooner or later. Repeatedly, the ancient culture presents us with customs that were acceptable at the time, but seem bizarre and immoral today. In the ancient Near East, polygamy was a legitimate way to prevent childlessness. The Bible offers numerous examples where a man added a second wife to overcome a first wife's barrenness. From a biological standpoint, this solution often worked. However, the human dynamics within a polygamous family were predictably disastrous.

Wealthier wives often preferred the option Sarah proposed, a type of surrogate motherhood involving the infertile woman's handmaid. Sarah's plan meant her husband would have sexual intercourse with her slave girl, Hagar. The child born of such a union legally belonged to the barren wife. The proposal seemed an ideal way for Sarah to overcome her barrenness, and she seemed driven to it by God's latest promise to Abraham: "a son coming *from your own body* will be your heir" (Genesis 15:4, emphasis added). This was a hair-raising prospect for an infertile, post-menopausal wife. Who was going to have Abraham's baby? According to Sarah's assessment, "The Lord has kept me from having children" (Genesis 16:2). Clearly this was Sarah's frantic last-ditch effort to salvage her honor as a woman and maintain a foothold in the promises of God.

Tragically, Abraham consented to Sarah's plan, Hagar became a disposable pawn in the scheme, and Sarah's faith hit an all-time low. The outcome was a disaster for Sarah and actually spread her pain to others. How could a plan that so completely disregarded (actually trampled) the dignity and rights of another of God's image bearers ever be considered a viable option?

Sometimes the honesty of the Bible is terribly disconcerting. These dark chapters from Sarah's life make us uncomfortable. It's hard to see someone like Sarah or Abraham, whom we consider to be "giants of the faith," toppled like large uprooted oak trees blasted by the hurricane winds of desperation, anxiety, and collapsing hopes.

Yet I often wonder how disheartening it would be for us if the Bible recorded only success stories. Would we ever understand how important the hard parts of life really are? Sarah—who in the New Testament is acclaimed as a woman of great faith—reminds us here how hard it is to trust God when everything is going wrong and hope is lost. The forces that assault our faith can be fierce. Even the strongest can stumble and fall. But in the end, Sarah's faith will be stronger and have deeper roots because of all she suffered.

We should also note that the choices confronting Sarah were complex and difficult. What should a woman do—how much will she sacrifice—when her husband's life is endangered? Besides, Sarah was Abraham's half sister. And what's wrong with pursuing a course of action or a philosophy that is widely accepted in your culture? No one would criticize her for giving her handmaiden to Abraham. It was a common practice.

Sarah's story highlights the kinds of awful moral dilemmas women often face. Walking with God doesn't spare us from hard choices, nor does it guarantee we'll always make the right choice. Our lives are full of well-intentioned mistakes and outright sin. Knowing God and our calling to bear his image sheds a guiding light on our path. Sarah had enormous responsibilities to God, to herself, and to others (as do we) to think carefully about the choices she was making and not to follow mindlessly the route approved by her husband or by her culture.

What course of action best reflects God's image? What path is consistent with faith in him and in his Word? What choice advances his cause in my life and in the lives of others? These are not easy questions to answer, although they are questions that can help us find our way.

Sarah could have left us with a powerful example of a woman guided by her faith in God, even though it meant taking a hard stand or letting go of her private hopes. But she didn't. Both of her choices pursued a path of faithlessness, and we cannot admire her or Abraham for their actions. With respect to Abraham's plot to protect himself from Pharaoh and King Abimelech and Sarah's strategy to produce an heir by Hagar, their actions were pragmatic and faithless, and the biblical narrator looks askance at what they did.

Sarah's scheme to gain a child through Hagar backfired horribly. Instead of a baby, she received Hagar's scorn. The slave girl, pregnant with Abraham's child, enjoyed one brief moment of triumph. She exalted herself over Sarah, who exploded with years of bottled-up outrage and pain. Sarah was so abusive to Hagar that the young girl feared for her life. After that, everything came unraveled. When the child was born, he was described as Abraham's son, not Sarah's. Abraham accepted Ishmael as the child of promise, and the door of hope slammed shut in Sarah's face.

GOD SPEAKS HER NAME

Thirteen years of silence followed. But God wasn't finished with Sarah. Abraham was ninety-nine and Sarah eighty-nine when God appeared again to Abraham. This time God proclaimed himself as El Shaddai—God Almighty—the sufficient, omnipotent, life-giving God who can and *will* fulfill his promises. God set the tone for this exchange when he said, *"As for me ..."* then told Abraham what he would do. He had brought this elderly couple to the point of fixed impossibility to show them that the promises rested on him alone.

Suddenly God's covenant seemed to expand in all directions, extending far beyond Abraham and his biological descendants, moving through time into eternity, and breaking through all sorts of barriers to achieve the impossible. Here God sets his people apart from everyone else by the seal of the covenant—circumcision—and also by their relationship with him. "Walk before me and be blameless.... *As for you*, you must keep my covenant, you and your descendants after you for the generations to come" (Genesis 17:1, 9, emphasis added).

Then, at long last, God spoke the name we have been longing to hear. *"As for Sarai* your wife, you are no longer to call her Sarai; her name will be Sarah. I will bless her and will surely give you a son by her. I will bless her so that she will be the mother of nations; kings of peoples will come from her" (Genesis 17:15–16, emphasis added). This announcement was so totally unexpected, not to mention outrageous, Abraham exploded with laughter and pled for Ishmael to inherit the blessing. God didn't laugh. He did not budge. Sarah will bear a son for Abraham. Abraham, it appears, kept this last preposterous detail to himself. Sarah had been through enough. Why raise her hopes that the sorrow and shame of childlessness might end at this late date?

CIRCUMCISION — THE SIGN OF THE COVENANT

I was in elementary school the first time I came across *circumcision* in my Bible. Since my father was a pastor, I figured he could explain the meaning of this strange new biblical word. I remember the moment I brought it up with him like it was yesterday, and probably so does he. We were riding along in the car—just the two of us—when I decided this was a good time to ask, "What is circumcision?" My dad was completely unprepared for his little girl to spring that question, which just goes to show how parents never know what a child will come up with next. His answer? "You'd better talk to your mother."

As an adult, the question I wanted to ask about circumcision wasn't "What?" but "Why?" Why would God introduce a sign of the covenant that seemed to exclude all the women? My puzzlement intensified when I read theology books that spoke of circumcision as the "entrance," or "welcome," of male infants into God's covenant. Frankly, I'm not sure how much a baby boy would appreciate that kind of welcome, but on a more personal level I could feel myself, along with every other young girl and woman, sliding to the margins of the page. Doesn't God welcome girls into his covenant too? Women wonder about this, and perhaps the delicacy of the subject matter makes it awkward (as it was with my dad) to bring it up. Still, we want to know *why* the sign of God's covenant was so male. What is God trying to tell us? Was his covenant for men only? Are men more important in his covenant than women?

If ever there was a place in the Bible where women seem to be swept aside, it is here. Surely Sarah felt this too. After years of feeling left out, this must have been the ultimate exclusion. I can imagine Sarah shaking her head in disbelief when she heard about this latest development. How lost can a woman get?

Once again, God knew exactly what he was doing. The rite of circumcision is rich with symbolism intended to distinguish God's people from the rest of the world. Circumcision teaches us our need for soul surgery—the radical, costly, and bloody process of removing our sin that Jesus accomplished when he bled and died for us on the cross. It is a reminder of the painful battle against sin and the awful price of victory—for God and for his people. But there is much, much more to the sign of God's covenant.

Circumcision takes us back to the beginning—back to God's great creation mandate to be fruitful and multiply. God was reiterating the glorious creation mandate to "be fruitful and multiply and fill the earth" in a way that included, but went beyond, the call to reproduce physically. When he first called Abraham out of Ur of the Chaldeans, God promised to make a great nation from Abraham's descendants. Now God revisits that subject and reveals the kind of nation he plans to produce through Abraham: a nation of people who walk with God. The rite of circumcision came with the call to "walk before me and be blameless ... you and your descendants after you for the generations to come."

Circumcision cuts in a man's flesh a permanent reminder of his call to walk with God. Through circumcision, Abraham affirmed his personal intention to walk with God and to do everything in his power to ensure that his children and their children after them followed the same path. Far from excluding women, the rite of circumcision made women indispensable. Obviously no man can reproduce physically by himself. But Abraham's need for Sarah went well beyond sexual intimacy and the physical birth of a child. According to God's word in Genesis, "It is not good for the man to be alone." Abraham needed Sarah's help for the bigger and even more impossible job of reproducing spiritually.

If God were trying to exalt men or show his preference for men over women, there were better, more visible ways of doing so. He could have made the sign of the covenant a symbol on the man's head—like a crown letting everyone know the man was chief, that he was supposed to do all the thinking, deciding, and leading. Or he could have marked the man's arm—symbolizing strength, power, and rule. Instead God chose circumcision, not as a symbol of manhood, but of intimacy, vulnerability, and fruitfulness. Circumcision spoke of a man's intimate relationship with his wife and of their union in reproducing children, both physically and spiritually.

Rather than being excluded, a woman could actually be represented *twice* by circumcision — first, as her father's descendant and one he guided to walk with God, and second, as a wife who united with her husband in fulfilling the call to raise up the next generation to follow God. By circumcising Abraham's household servants too, God's covenant broke the boundaries of biology, extending the Abrahamic covenant laterally to encompass Gentiles even at this early stage. Both Abraham and Sarah had responsibility to direct the hearts of their servants and their servants' children toward God. Circumcision wasn't *male*-centered, but *descendant*-centered and *community*-centered. The sign of the covenant impressed upon the man his enormous spiritual responsibility to walk before God and be faithful and to influence others, especially those under his roof, to do the same. This burden was too great for any man to shoulder alone. Sarah, the *ezer*, would join him in battling for the souls of the next generation.

TALKING WITH GOD THROUGH A TENT DOOR

Sarah's day finally came. This time the Lord appeared as a man with two other men (angels, presumably). Following custom, Abraham hosted these three mysterious guests. As a married woman, Sarah remained out of sight, secluded in the tent, but stealthily within earshot of the men's conversation — which makes me love her all the more. For the first time, the Lord (who knew she was listening) spoke to Sarah by talking with Abraham. Before the conversation was over, the Lord was talking directly to her.

One can imagine the mixture of emotions that ran through Sarah as she heard the Lord speak her name and promise a son to her. Who can blame her for laughing to herself? What a joke. Sarah was about to learn that she didn't have a private life. She never had. The one on the other side of the tent door knew she laughed, knew her incredulity, also knew all about her sorrow and her unbelief.

Sarah was so defeated by her circumstances, *she* had forgotten God. He brought her to the end of her hopes to bring her to himself. And so he asked a question, which on the surface seems completely absurd, but which in truth was utterly profound, "Why did Sarah laugh?" (Genesis 18:13). Why? Because it was hopeless—utterly ridiculous—to think an old woman who was unable to conceive when she was young could conceive life now that her insides were shriveled up and dead. Anyone would laugh at the thought. The second question the Lord asked would play over and over again in her mind until the day she died: "Is anything too hard for the LORD?" (Genesis 18:14).

A LIFE ON HOLD

Sarah's life was a long torturous journey from "The LORD has kept me from having children" (Genesis 16:2) to the miracle birth of Isaac and the day she rejoiced, saying, "God has brought me laughter" (Genesis 21:6). Her laughter had been a long time coming. After delivering a son at the ripe old age of ninety, she had solid physical evidence that *nothing* is too hard for the Lord. It was a beautiful and fitting climax to the long, weary road Sarah had traveled.

But to be honest, that joyful moment isn't the part of Sarah's life that touches me most. While there are rich lessons to be gathered from God's ability to create life in a dead womb, the long, drawn-out silent stretch that took up most of her life is the part of her story that both fascinates and disturbs me. It's also the part that looks most familiar. There's wisdom to be gained in freezing Sarah's story right in the middle, before the part about Hagar and the astonishing words she heard the Lord speak through the tent door.

If the truth were known, that's where I spend most of my time—stuck somewhere in the middle, longing to see God's hand, trying to find my place in his purposes, struggling to put one foot in front of the other and keep moving. Daily confronted by my helplessness to change those things that trouble me most, there's no escaping the fact that while nothing is too hard for the Lord, he's not afraid to keep me waiting.

What are we to make of this? How do we go on when some major piece of our lives is missing or broken? Are we to put our lives on hold and wait for him finally to come through for us? Is that how we're supposed to live? How much of our lives do we let slip away while we drum our fingers restlessly waiting to graduate, get married, have a baby, buy a house, or get that big break at work? What do we do in those long stretches when life comes to a standstill because of God's silence, when day after day we're looking at the same problems, the same unchanged heart, the same unhealed body?

I keep hoping and praying for that miracle. But the problem I wrestle with most is how to live in the silence. Sarah's eighty-nine years is an awfully long time to wait before discovering God's purpose for your life. Caught in God's silence, "We cannot see the end from the middle and must walk by faith, not by sight."[1] It's the hardest thing we ever do. Sometimes I think there's more to learn from Sarah's failures than from her eleventh-hour triumph.

Sarah made a lot of mistakes. She put her life on hold. She watched a lot of precious years slip away believing she had failed as a woman. After all, a *real* woman gives her husband sons. Even her identity as a wife was stolen away at her husband's urging. God didn't seem to want her life. Sarah didn't see a place for herself in the big things God was doing for Abraham. There was nothing to write about her in the family Christmas letter. Had God benched Sarah until the final play of the game, or was she part of the team all along?

ALL IN THE FAMILY

A little girl—around the age of four or five—was adopted into a rather large family. As she began settling into the love of her new family and adjusting to her new surroundings, she often went to the wall in the house where photographs of all the other family members were on display. She would stand there for long periods of time silently studying their faces. Soon after her arrival, her mother took her daughter to the photographer. The mother told me later she wasn't sure her little one fully comprehended the significance of that outing until days later when she came in from play and her mother sent her to look at the wall. When the little girl saw her own picture hanging there with the rest of the family, she laughed and sobbed at the same time.

If Sarah had gone to God's family wall, she would have found her portrait hanging alongside her brothers. It had been there all along. If she thought her frame was empty until the day she had a baby, she couldn't have been more mistaken. Sarah was part of God's family, a true daughter—not an in-law—born to bear God's image, born to advance his cause. Her identity as a woman was anchored to God, and nothing could ever take that away from her. She was encircled in his love every bit as much as Abraham, only she was so distracted by her barrenness, she couldn't see how much she mattered to God.

Amazingly, Sarah was the *first* person to taste the blessings of God's covenant. Pharaoh learned to his dismay that Sarah was the apple of God's eye. God lashed out against the Egyptian ruler's household with a terrible plague "because of Abram's wife Sarai" (Genesis 12:17). Later, God's threatening words to Abimelech, "You are as good as dead" (Genesis 20:3), sent this chilling, unambiguous message: Lay a hand on Sarah and you will reckon with God.

Sarah also had a crucial role to play in God's purposes. Her obvious contribution was, of course, the birth of Isaac—not just any ordinary son, but the son of promise. Sarah gave birth to the child whose family line would ultimately lead to Jesus, the Redeemer promised in Eden. But Sarah had other vital contributions too.

She was an *ezer*—joined in a "bone-of-my-bones" union with Abraham. Her first (but not her only) calling was to soldier alongside Abraham, wherever God led them. In God's eyes, a husband and a wife are *one*. His call to one of them entails, by necessity, a calling for the other. It works both ways. When God called Abraham and gave him promises, Sarah had her marching orders too. And when Sarah anguished over her inability to conceive, God called Abraham to enter wholeheartedly into her struggle with God, not to watch and give pointers from the sidelines.

Even before they left Ur, Sarah was already on active duty. An *ezer* is always on duty. She and Abraham were barely on their way before there was a crucial need for her to act. One wonders how differently their story would read if, instead of cooperating with Abraham's cowardly plot and lying about their marriage, Sarah had reminded him God had promised protection from his enemies and firmly refused to go along with his request? What if, instead of victimizing Hagar, she had shielded her slave girl and entrusted her own destiny to God? These are questions no one can answer, but they help us see that no matter what shape our lives are in or what we may lack in the eyes of others or even in our own eyes, we have a crucial role in God's purposes and vital ministries to offer others.

Instead of drawing her identity and purpose from God, Sarah fell into the same trap that catches the rest of us. She listened to the voices of her culture, her circumstances, and the people around her who were telling her who she was, what would make her life fulfilling, and how she could contribute.

We hear voices too, telling us we're missing out or deficient as women if we're alone or childless, if our families aren't perfect or our home isn't featured in *Better Homes and Gardens*. Even women who enjoy the single life and love their careers get lost in a world of couples and families and frequent reminders that they're somehow incomplete. Those messages come from the secular culture and, sadly, even from well-meaning Christian friends and leaders in the church. They do not speak for God. We are his daughters, and our completeness comes from him.)

Despite her failings (which ought to endear her to us more than if she were some paragon of perfection), Sarah left behind a strong legacy of faith and a powerful message for the church. We have Sarah to thank for teaching us, through her long heartbreaking and ultimately hopeless quest for a child, an invaluable lesson about God's limitless power. Her marathon wait for a child into old age and her geriatric pregnancy leave us with a vivid impression of God's power to create life where there is no hope. "Is anything too hard for the Lord?" ⟩ NO

God wasn't promising more twilight pregnancies for women or that the impossibility that confronts us now will turn out exactly as we hope. His question to Sarah wasn't a blank check for us to cash in any way we choose. Through Sarah, he demonstrated in the strongest possible way that he will always keep his promises, and *nothing* can stand in his way. God is still building the great nation he promised through Abraham—a people from all nations who walk faithfully with God.) Sarah reminds us of God's promises and of his power to keep his word. He enables us to be fruitful and to multiply, too, in building his church, even though we are weak in faith, our best efforts seem fruitless, and the souls we long most to win seem hopelessly hardened to the gospel. We can take heart and hold onto hope, for *nothing* is too hard for the Lord.)

In the end, God gave Sarah a promise and her faith in him grew strong. By faith, she mustered courage and strength at the ripe old age of eight-nine to try one last time to conceive a child. The New Testament rightly honors Sarah. "By faith even Sarah herself received ability to conceive, even beyond the proper time of life, since she considered Him faithful who had promised" (Hebrews 11:11 NASB).

Sarah reassures us that we have a vital place in God's purposes, that he values us and is at work in our lives. But some might think Sarah was an exception; after all, she was Abraham's first lady and a woman of prominence and privilege. Of course *she* mattered to God.

What if we don't see ourselves in that elite category? Hagar takes us to the other side of the tracks—to a place called hopeless—where in utter desolation she probes the outer boundaries of God's heart for women. Her story takes us to the bottom of the heap of humanity, where Hagar is lost inside her own skin.

FOCUS: Sarah struggled to secure her place in God's purposes, as life passed her by and her hopes of bearing the child of promise expired. We will learn through Sarah's story that even when it looks like we're missing out on the big things God is doing, we have a high calling and a vital mission to carry out every day of our lives.

SARAH'S STORY: Genesis 11:27–32; 12:1–13:4; 15:1–5; 16:1–6, 15–16; 17:1–27; 18:1–15; 20:1–18; 21:1–13; 23:1–20

FOR DISCUSSION, READ: Genesis 11:26–31; 18:1–15

1. Describe a time when you felt God's silence in your life.

2. How did you interpret God's silence? What did you think about God? About yourself?

3. How did God's silence impact Sarah?

4. What did she believe she needed to do to have a place in God's purposes? How did that belief affect her as well as her relationships with God and with others?

5. How did the fact that God created Sarah to be his image bearer and an *ezer* mean that her place in his purposes was already secure?

6. How did Sarah's focus on bearing a son distract her from her mission to be Abraham's spiritual ally and to reflect God's image in her relationship with Hagar?

7. How did Sarah and Abraham fail as a Blessed Alliance? How did they succeed?

8. When we're living in God's silence, how do we get sidetracked from our true mission?

THE INVISIBLE
WOMAN—

Hagar

*G*irls *are not important. They do not count.*"
You might expect to hear that kind of anti-female rhetoric around an elementary schoolyard—the Tom Sawyer nastiness that irks little girls and prompts adults to wink philosophically. After all, "boys will be boys." This remark, however, didn't come from a worked-up adolescent taunting his female classmates. Nor was it a cocky adolescent team captain's rationale for preferring boys over girls when choosing sides for a game. This was the calm, matter-of-fact conviction of a grown man, an Afghan soldier, who was talking about his own sisters. He meant exactly what he said.[1]

The war in Afghanistan touched us all. One of the most shocking cultural differences to parade across our TV screens was how harshly women were treated under the Taliban. Americans on the political right and left were horrified to see women imprisoned in what looked to us like a "body bag for the living." We were intrigued and appalled by those faceless blue shapes that seemed to be everywhere in Afghanistan. What was it like to view life through the mesh of the blue burkas the Taliban regime compelled women to wear? In their culture, it was a fact of life—"Girls do not count."

We may pride ourselves that in the more enlightened and progressive West we've moved beyond such primitive attitudes. But even here that same message has a way of getting through to us. Do women count? We have our doubts when we hear one of those tasteless jokes or wisecracks about women—"just meant in fun." The notion resides in our pocketbooks when we bring home lower pay than men for doing the same job. We wonder secretly in the church when women's gifts and ministries are valued less than men's or when "kingdom work" is portrayed in manly terms and located outside the home. It hits us hardest when we're going through some personal crisis where we feel like a prop in someone else's story or when God himself seems too busy helping others to pay much attention to us. Let's be honest. Many of us, when we stop to consider our place in the world (not just in Afghanistan), have wondered at one time or another, Do I really count?

DROPPING BELOW ZERO

In the case of Hagar, Sarah's handmaid, there was no debate. Hagar did not count. Perhaps in another place and time, or under different circumstances, she might have received a little more respect from others and had a better opinion of herself. In the Bible, however, by the time she enters the story, she is already at rock bottom. Sarah, we are told, "had an Egyptian maidservant named Hagar." Hagar was a slave.

We tend to read those simple and direct words about Hagar without emotion. However, those same words would evoke bitter emotions in Hagar. She was a lost soul right from the start—stuck on the wrong side of the racial divide, uncomfortable inside her own skin, and trapped within a cultural system that stripped her of her rights, her dignity, and her freedom. I fear contemporary Christians have added insult to her injuries by allowing her to lie flat on the pages of our Bibles as some lifeless cardboard character. She seems so small and insignificant, almost invisible, alongside the larger figures in her story—the legendary Abraham and Sarah. She's a messy complication in the major plot involving her mistress. The loss is mostly ours, for in losing Hagar, a powerful healing message that women hunger for today quietly slips through our fingers.

If the childless Sarah scored a zero in the ancient culture, Hagar fell into the minus column. Although she shared with Sarah the disadvantages every woman experienced in the patriarchal culture, Hagar was far more vulnerable. She was an Egyptian, a Gentile, a foreigner. Hagar was on the outside looking in. Her gender and her race alone were enough to complicate her life. But these were minor compared to her social status as a slave.

Most biblical scholars believe Hagar entered the Genesis narrative anonymously several chapters earlier when Pharaoh was enriching Abraham for the privilege of marrying his "sister" Sarah. Pharaoh treated Abraham well for Sarah's sake, giving him "sheep and cattle, male and female donkeys, menservants and *maidservants*, and camels" (Genesis 12:16, emphasis added). Hagar may well have been an item on the inventory of property that changed hands between Pharaoh and Abraham. What a horror to wake up one morning to the news that you're heading for the auction block, that before the day is out you'll be wrenched from the people you know and love, degraded by being lined up with cattle and other livestock, and placed in the hands of a stranger. In his writings, the former American slave Frederick Douglass relived that dehumanizing experience from his personal history:

> Men and women, young and old, married and single; moral and
> intellectual beings, in open contempt of their humanity, leveled

at a blow with horses, sheep, horned cattle and swine! Horses and men—cattle and women—pigs and children—all holding the same rank in the scale of social existence; and all subjected to the same narrow inspection, to ascertain their value in gold and silver—the only standard of worth applied by slaveholders to slaves![2]

The kinds of flashbacks a slave would have were as bad as any post-war trauma suffered by military veterans. To give a small taste of how bad it could get, another former slave described nightmarish images of powerlessness, heartless haggling over family members, and the crushing and often permanent separations from precious loved ones.

My brothers and sisters were bid off first, and one by one, while my mother, paralyzed with grief, held me by the hand. Her turn came and she was bought by Isaac Riley of Montgomery County. Then I was offered.... My mother, half distracted with the thought of parting forever from all her children, pushed through the crowd while the bidding for me was going on, to the spot where Riley was standing. She fell at his feet, and clung to his knees, entreating him in tones that a mother could only command, to buy her baby as well as herself, and spare to her one, at least, of her little ones.... This man disengaged himself from her with ... violent blows and kicks.... I must have been then between five and six years old.[3]

Like the slaves in America's history, Hagar was an African slave. How she became a slave, no one will ever know. Was she a "spoil" of war, or was she stolen away by some other method? Did her parents sell her to cover their indebtedness? Was she born into slavery as the child of slaves? Was she torn from her weeping mother's arms? The only surviving piece of demographics regarding Hagar was her Egyptian nationality. Other than that, there is nothing. She was cut off from family, friends, her country, even from her private history. Utterly alone in the world, with no one to speak out for her or to protect her from harm, Hagar faced a life sentence of catering to the biddings of others, caring for the wealthy, and serving their whims. Who was looking after Hagar? nobody

THE INVISIBLE WOMAN

regno

Hagar was human property and did not even have rights over her own body. Those rights belonged to another. One can only imagine what went through Hagar's mind when she was told of Sarah's plan to use her as a surrogate mother. Sarah, as far as we can tell, showed no regard for Hagar's human dignity or acknowledged that her handmaid had the same feelings, hopes, and longings as any other woman. The young slave girl was nothing more than Sarah's last chance of becoming a mother. Sarah added to Hagar's job description the task of bearing a child by her aging husband.

This revolting situation is slightly tempered, from our twenty-first-century point of view at least, if we keep Hagar's picture in its ancient frame. In her day, the prevalence of polygamy meant multiple wives and concubines were commonplace. They were often a necessity to preserve and build a family, especially where the primary wife was barren. No doubt a lot of young women grew up knowing they would inevitably land in one of those "secondary" slots in a household. Furthermore, modern notions of independence and individualism were completely foreign to the ancient mind. Fathers arranged marriages, often for the benefit of the family. Sometimes a daughter's wishes were consulted (for example when Rebekah married Isaac, Genesis 24). More often, the decision was out of a young woman's hands (sometimes even out of a young man's), as fathers negotiated and arranged the marriages of their children. Sarah's actions wouldn't have seemed quite so outrageous in the ancient Near East—although this doesn't make the reproductive assignment any less hurtful to Hagar.

It is important (and encouraging) that the biblical narrator regards the actions of Sarah and Abraham with deep disapproval. Viewed from heaven's perspective, the scene is filled with darkness and chaos. It's almost a replay of the moment Eve "took" and ate the fruit, then "gave" some to her husband. The narrator employs the same language. Sarah "*took* her Egyptian maidservant Hagar and *gave* her to her husband to be his wife. He slept with Hagar, and she [Sarah's Egyptian slave girl] conceived" (Genesis 16:3–4, emphasis added).

Viewed from Sarah's perspective, this was a culturally acceptable course of action. Some even believe Sarah may have been obligated or duty bound to step aside and let a younger woman do what she was incapable of doing, namely, conceive a child for her husband. Ancient Near Eastern laws actually authorized a barren wife to use her maidservant in this capacity. What is worse, these laws stipulated that afterward, the child belonged to the barren woman, who then had the power to sell or keep her maidservant. The law was on Sarah's side. Hagar was alone and had no voice.

Viewed from Hagar's perspective, the whole affair only underscored her insignificance as a person. She had no meaning or value in herself. She was beneficial to Sarah and Abraham only because she was capable of making a baby. As a person, Hagar was invisible. No one anticipated how the dynamics between the two women would explode when Sarah's scheme succeeded. As it turned out, Hagar's "pride and her mistress's antagonism" placed the two women on a collision course.[4]

THE PRICE OF PERSONHOOD

In a slightly strange way, Hagar reminds me of a Saudi woman I used to observe in Oxford who was covered from head to ankle in a coal-black burka. Oxford is in many ways an international crossroads. Walking around town on errands when we were living there, I passed women whose dress revealed the country they were from. This Saudi woman was usually pushing a stroller containing her small child, as she made her way down the road at breakneck speed. I learned from watching her—this woman whose name I didn't know and whose face I never saw—that it takes a lot to squelch the spirit of a woman. Below the hem of her mandatory burka, glistening defiantly as she raced along, was a pair of fiery red patent leather shoes.)

Hagar had lots of reasons to feel beaten down, but when she discovered she was pregnant, one might say, she put on her fiery red patent leather shoes. Although her legal status was unchanged, her social standing was transformed. She succeeded where Sarah failed. She conceived a child. Not only was she validated as a woman by her pregnancy, she was carrying Abraham's offspring. Though her actions proved unwise, risky, and heartlessly insensitive, it was perhaps an indication of Hagar's strong spirit that her triumph led her to scorn the barren Sarah.

The wounded older woman lashed out with a vengeance against her insolent maid. How ironic that Sarah was oblivious to the wrongs she had committed against Hagar, yet acutely sensitive to Hagar's offense against her. This troubling picture is worthy of sober reflection, when we remember the Word of God is a mirror that reflects our own souls. Sarah described Hagar's contempt against her as "violence"—the same word that described conditions in the world before the great flood.[5] Her handmaid's unguarded moment of triumph was short-lived, for Sarah unleashed such fury against her handmaid that the younger woman feared for her life. Abraham was passive in the face of this family crisis, which caused the cycle of wrongs to spiral wildly out of control. Hagar was the mother of his child and deserved his protection, but he did not give it. Sarah, his wife of many years, was in indescribable pain and actually turned to Abraham for intervention. But instead of working to establish peace in his divided home by seeking God's help, giving godly guidance and reassurance to Sarah, and by restraining Hagar from any further incident, Abraham offered little more than a shrug. To Sarah, he said, "Your servant is in your hands. Do with her whatever you think best" (Genesis 16:6). His withdrawal opened the door for Sarah's harsh mistreatment of Hagar, who fled for her life into the wilderness in the general direction of Egypt. Truly a black moment in the history of the chosen family. And the Blessed Alliance sinks to new lows in the whole Hagar episode of the Abraham story. Instead of working together to advance God's purposes, God's people are in disarray, inflicting injuries upon one another.

THE WOMAN AT THE WELL

In a strange twist of fate, the crisis that appeared to signal the end of Hagar's life was in fact the real beginning. Like the rejected Samaritan woman (John 4) who found her life when she encountered Jesus at Jacob's well, so Hagar found her life near a spring of water in the first of two encounters with the Angel of the Lord.

Historically, the church has always held that these Old Testament appearances of the Angel of the Lord—and there are several—were actually pre-incarnate appearances of the Son of God. Usually in these encounters, a person didn't realize at first who they were actually seeing. Only as the conversation progressed (and sometimes only after it was over) did it dawn on them that they had seen the Angel of the Lord. What this divine encounter will do for Hagar is difficult to quantify, but many believe this is when Hagar embraced the God of Abraham. She was in great peril—pregnant, afflicted, humiliated, frightened, and alone. Her sense of herself and of her value as a human being had bottomed out.

The Angel's encounter with Hagar gives an early hint of Paul's word to the Galatians, that "there is neither Jew nor [Gentile], slave nor free, male nor female, for you are all one in Christ

Jesus" (Galatians 3:28). Hagar was disenfranchised on all three counts, for she was a Gentile, a slave, and a woman. She came to this moment as Sarah's abused and rejected slave girl. But to the Angel of the Lord she was God's image bearer with great value, dignity, and purpose.

When one pulls back the temporal veil, the modern reader can see that Hagar matters deeply to God. She may have been invisible to everyone else, but she was neon bright on God's radar screen. This wilderness meeting was no chance encounter. "The angel of the LORD *found* Hagar" (Genesis 16:7, emphasis added), the finding that comes from searching and seeking. She may have been running to escape injury or death with no clear idea of where she was going. But the terror that drove her into the wilderness drove her into the safe arms of the Angel. This rendezvous would utterly transform the life of a hopeless and unloved slave girl.

"Hagar, servant of Sarai, where have you come from, and where are you going?" (Genesis 16:8). In the Bible, Abraham and Sarah never addressed Hagar by name, but the Angel of the Lord called her name and knew everything about her. We can only imagine what such recognition meant to her. This is the perfect moment when we might expect the Angel of the Lord to emancipate Hagar from slavery, to change her rags into a beautiful gown and give her a life of her own. Instead, he does the opposite. He sends her back. "Go back to your mistress and submit to her," literally, "put yourself under her hand." If we truly grasp what drove Hagar out into the wilderness, these are harsh and terrifying instructions—not at all the way her instincts were leading her. But God calls his children to do things his way, and that often means going against the grain of our own hearts.

For Hagar, it meant returning to a situation that was both miserable and dangerous. This was not some suicidal plan of action—some self-inflicted martyrdom—locking Hagar into a hopelessly degrading situation. Certainly the Angel's message for Hagar should *never* be interpreted as a reason for anyone to return to an abusive situation. The specifics of Hagar's case are unusual, and God's purposes here are redemptive. He addressed the *ezer* in her, involved her in his purposes, and gave her a mission that required her to go back. Hagar's fledgling faith in God enabled her to obey.

This dejected woman heard from God that she and her unborn child were included in God's promises to Abraham. She was not peripheral to God's plan for Abraham or for Sarah—a strong hint that God intended all along to encompass Gentiles among his people. God had a plan for Hagar too. She learned she was carrying a son and that both she and her child would survive their tragedy. She was to return to her master and tell him God had named their son Ishmael. But she was bringing to Abraham and Sarah a whole lot more than this piece of prophetic news.

In her encounter with the Angel of God, Hagar received dignity and meaning. The simple but unchanging truth that God's eyes were fixed on her empowered her with a kind of freedom no one could ever take away. She was not alone. She *did* matter. This freed her to do the extraordinary—to love her neighbor, to put the interests of others ahead of herself (Philippians 2:3–4), and to reflect the image of God in her relationships.

God has always been in the business of changing lives. He calls his children to live in a radically different way than the rest of the world, so that it shocks us when we see Hagar returning to live as his image bearer in a difficult and uncertain situation. As with the Samaritan woman, Hagar will never be the same after her encounter with the Lord. He raised her actions to a new and higher level of significance. By serving Sarah, Hagar knows she is serving God.

HAGAR, THE THEOLOGIAN

At this early stage, Hagar's theology is elemental. But she has absorbed enough from this brief encounter with the Angel of the

Lord to face what lies ahead. Her next two actions reveal what real theology is all about. First, she does the unthinkable. *She* gives God a name. No one else in Scripture—male or female—ever names God. Hagar does. She names him El Roi: "the God who sees me." The new name she gives to God expresses her most basic theological conviction: she is not invisible to God.

Second, Hagar *lived* her theology—took it with her into the hardest place of all. Knowing God's eye was upon her emboldened her to do the impossible. She returned to Sarah, the woman she most feared and who had grievously wronged her. After years of slavery, Hagar's return to Sarah was possibly the first truly free act of her life. Sarah thought she needed Hagar to secure a baby for her husband. Now Hagar has something Sarah needs a whole lot more than a child—the message that God's eyes are on Sarah too. He sees, not as a disinterested spectator who just happens to have super vision, but with the concerned involvement and understanding of a loving parent who has a lot at stake in whatever happens to his child.

The thirteen years of silence that follow the birth of Ishmael—Abraham's son—seem to indicate a measure of peace in Abraham's household after Hagar's return. One scholar speculates that this silence could be a hint that Abraham was finally protecting Hagar. I'd like to think the explanation is that Hagar took the initiative in making peace with Sarah. Of course, no one will ever know.

POCKET THEOLOGY FOR THE UNSEEN AND UNLOVED

Hagar has done for theology what Palm Pilots have done for computers—she made it personal. Before Hagar's encounter with the Angel of the Lord, God is spoken of in large, majestic, sweeping terms as Elohim, the creator God, the judge of all the earth, Yahweh (or Jehovah) the covenant maker, the promise keeper, Shaddai (the Almighty), but not in the intimately personal terms that

Hagar used. Hagar advanced theology by revealing the intimate side of God. He is the God who never takes his eye off of his child. This was a truth that Abraham and Sarah needed to hear.

Hagar introduced God's people to the doctrine of God's omniscience—not simply that God knows everything, but that *he knows me*. Later, King David expanded this intimate view of God in his beautifully comforting Psalm 139: "Oh LORD, you have searched *me* and you know *me*" (emphasis added). Jesus took things even further when he taught his followers to call God by his family name, "Abba," or "Papa"—the affectionate language of a little child who crawls up in her father's lap.

Professional theologians can write many pages in their systematic theology volumes about the doctrine of God's omniscience (pages well worth reading, by the way) in terms that sometimes sound grandiose and don't always touch down in such personal ways. Hagar took this staggering concept—that God knows everything about me—and made it compact enough to fit inside her pocket. "You are the God who sees me." Invisible to Abraham and Sarah, now Hagar lived in the warmth of God's gaze. So far as she was concerned, nothing would ever be the same.

It helps a little to know that Hagar was now on a mission, that she possessed vital information about God's promises and about his character that Abraham and Sarah needed to know. Her story became part of the family heritage—the oral tradition that got passed from one generation to the next until Moses committed it to writing. Still, considering the risks, it boggles the mind that the Angel sent her back. It was so pointless when her unborn son Ishmael wasn't ultimately to be the son of promise and it was just a matter of time before Sarah and Abraham expelled Hagar and her child again. This was a losing enterprise for Hagar. Are we seeing just another round of benefits for Abraham and Sarah at Hagar's expense, or did God have anything in this for Hagar?

In her wilderness encounter with the Angel of the Lord, God gave Hagar two gifts. The first was the priceless discovery of the knowledge that God was watching her, that she mattered to him, even if she didn't matter to another soul. Here was a priceless truth she would reach for again and again in the days ahead. His second gift didn't come wrapped in bright paper with a bow, but was priceless just the same. In sending her back to Abraham and Sarah, God was blessing Hagar again. God doesn't call us to himself without also calling us to his people. It is a mixed blessing for all of us, for the church isn't always the safest place. The people there aren't necessarily the ones we would choose for our friends, and, sadly, some of our most painful wounds come from our relationships with other believers. But these are the people we need and who also need us. We come to know God better and grow stronger as Christians when we are joined to the community of his people and we work together to know him.

Hagar had only begun to know her great God. She had so much more to learn, and there was so much she needed to understand. It puts things in perspective, even in light of Hagar's ultimate ejection, to realize God was sending her back to the two people best equipped to help her learn more about him. Only imagine what you could learn if you spent over fifteen years around Abraham and Sarah. Hagar would hear about the promises. She would learn the teachings Abraham passed on to Ishmael. Hagar had a front row seat for the spectacular birth of Isaac—the fulfillment of God's promise. But it was a two-way street. Hagar expanded their understanding of God too. She will always be best known for helping God's people—then and now—understand in such an intimate way that God sees me.

LESSONS FROM A SLAVE

In the very complexity of our lives, Hagar is also one of the best arguments for the importance of a vital practical theology for women. Whenever I talk to women's groups, I'm always taken aback by the impact of Hagar's message on women. I can talk about a hundred other things, but when I'm finished, what they carry away in their pockets is a simple: "God sees me"—not as one of a sea of faces that he observes when his eyes scan the earth, but "me" all by myself, as though he had no one else to think about but me.

It just goes to show how lonely life can be amid the hustle and bustle of activities, errands, crowds, and friendships. Even inside a good marriage or close friendship, there's still a dimension of isolation we can't escape. For all of us there are plenty of wilderness experiences when we suffer symptoms of isolation and insignificance. For all of us, there are inevitable moments when, even surrounded by loving family and friends, we feel invisible or go through something alone. A surgery, a divorce, a death, a failure. Those sleepless nights, those closet moments, those tears we shed in private. What we wouldn't give to find Hagar's spring and to be found by the Angel of the Lord.

Hagar has more to teach us. Her story levels a devastating blow against anyone who tries to make the case that women don't count or that we are second-class citizens in God's kingdom. God simply couldn't have made a stronger statement of how much he values women and how central they are to what he is doing. Who can argue when God gives a woman like Hagar—a disenfranchised slave girl who is clinging to the bottom rung of the human ladder and utterly alone in life—this kind of one-on-one personal attention? God focuses on Hagar despite the fact that the child she carries is *not* the promised one and her story is only a messy interruption to the *real* story God is weaving. Yet he treats Hagar like she's the most important person in the world as he follows her into the wilderness to affirm his love for her and bring a sudden and permanent end to her aloneness.

God invests Hagar—along with other women—with enormous significance when he entrusts her with the revelation of new elements of the Abrahamic covenant. God might repeat the covenant to others. But here he *expands* it in a private appearance to an unknown outsider, an Egyptian, a slave, and a woman. Many men in Scripture who secured more significant roles in the drama of redemptive history *never* had an encounter like this. Nor did any of the major matriarchs in Abraham's family.

Furthermore, Hagar was an early developer of Christian theology. Her life unveiled a side of God that was truly revolutionary. Up to this point, not even Abraham or Sarah talked about God in such intimate terms. Where would Christianity be if we were left with the impressions of Abraham and Sarah—of a God who speaks with grandiose promises and leaves you with more questions than answers; a God who talks to women as an aside through a tent door while he's conversing and dining with the men? There were hints of God's love and intimate involvement in the lives of certain major individuals before now, but through Hagar our understanding of God takes a giant leap forward. We gained a jaw-dropping sense of God's intimate interest and care for each person when one of the "little people" of human history got a raw deal. No one had experienced a caring close-up like this before.

As a final reminder, the power of Hagar's message for us would be thoroughly diluted if she had lived in another place and time. But against the backdrop of the patriarchal culture—where women were marginalized and the value of a slave as a person was below zero—the message of Hagar's story packs a stronger punch. Given the bigness of Abraham and the smallness of this young slave girl, this story shouts out loudly to Hagar and all of God's daughters: "Girls *do* count."

Next we will consider a woman who made sure she counted, but until recently has been routinely discounted as one of the "bad girls" of the Bible. In the opinion of many, Tamar was lost in more ways than one, and there are many who might consider the value of recovering her questionable at best.

FOCUS: The slave girl Hagar had a whole list of reasons for thinking she was invisible. It was easy to conclude from the way her life was going that she didn't matter to anyone. Her encounter with El Roi—"the God who sees me"—turned her around. Hagar teaches us a powerful lesson of just how profoundly important we are to God.

HAGAR'S STORY: Genesis 16:1–16; 21:8–21

FOR DISCUSSION, READ: Genesis 16:1–16

1. How was Hagar lost? What made her invisible?

2. Do you relate to Hagar's sense that she really didn't matter? Why?

3. How did Hagar's experiences with Sarah reinforce her sense that she didn't matter?

4. Why did the encounter with the Angel of the Lord change Hagar's perspective? *Salvation*

5. What gave Hagar the courage to return to Sarah? *God's love*

6. What was Hagar's mission in returning? Beyond giving birth to a son, what significant contributions did Hagar make to Abraham and Sarah's understanding of God? *more personal*

7. Why is Hagar a remarkable figure in biblical history? Why is her significance both unlikely and surprising, yet a perfect example of how God often works through women?

8. How is Hagar's story an encouragement to you?

MISSING IN ACTION—

Tamar

"*W*omen corrupted the line of Christ!*"*

Knowing the history behind some of the men named in Jesus' family tree, I could hardly believe the words coming from the pulpit. I have heard more than one sermon on the women in Matthew's genealogy,[1] and I always wait for someone to take note of how unusual it was to include women in ancient lineages and to unpack the significance of listing them in Matthew. Occasionally I am pleasantly surprised. More often, I hear the kind of criticism this pastor was leveling. No doubt with commentaries to back him up, he was simply stating the obvious, or so he thought, given the fact that the only women mentioned—Tamar, Rahab, Ruth, and Bathsheba—were four Gentiles best known for their sexual escapades.

These women got lost because of their shady actions. It's hard for a lot of people to see them under any other light. Perhaps, as some have suggested, Matthew included their names as an encouraging reminder that God's grace is far-reaching and even includes such disreputable and unlikely candidates as these. But maybe he had better reasons for breaking the rules by inserting the names of four women in a list that normally included only men.

Rahab got her start as a Canaanite prostitute in Jericho. Even after forsaking prostitution, risking her life to embrace the God of Israel, marrying into the most respectable family in Judah, and raising Boaz (a son to make any mother proud), she never succeeded in shedding her original identity as a harlot.

Ruth the Moabitess, one of our all-time favorites, still worries us a little. We're not exactly sure what she was up to in the middle of the night when she sidled up to the sleeping Boaz on the threshing floor and "uncovered his feet."

Bathsheba's reputation was tarnished for good by her adulterous affair with King David—a sordid chapter in David's past that might never have happened if she hadn't been bathing within view of his balcony.

And what can anyone say in defense of Tamar—a brassy woman who took things into her own hands, stooped to impersonate a prostitute, and seduced her own father-in-law?

The belief that there's a temptress inside every woman leaps out into the open in opinions held of this infamous quartet. As soon as anything of a sexual nature occurs, the woman involved becomes the prime suspect. She bears more of the blame and carries the guilt a whole lot longer than the man involved. We associate King David with a heart for God, godly music and poetry, youthful heroics against Goliath, his aboveboard conduct toward the unscrupulous King Saul, and his lifelong dream of building God's temple. Mention Bathsheba, however, and the first and often the only thing that springs to mind is her immoral liaison with the king. It's disheartening to see just how unredemptive and one-sided our memories can be.

A COLD CASE

Twice widowed in sequence by Judah's eldest two sons, the childless Tamar is notorious for deceiving Judah, who impregnated her without realizing the mysterious prostitute he hired was his own daughter-in-law. Tamar's story is one of those passages parents skip over when reading the Bible to their children and probably ranks among the top ten passages in the Bible that pastors tend to avoid as well. The subject matter hardly seems suitable for a general audience, and trying to find some redeeming practical application for a congregation is a challenge.

Tamar's alleged motive was her desperation to have a child—a motive that hardly justifies such outrageous and unorthodox behavior. Because of her "deceptive trickery" of the revered tribal head of Israel's royal line, Tamar has for generations born the brunt of negative remarks about the women Matthew names in Jesus' genealogy, especially because her actions sound a bit cold-blooded and vindictive, not to mention immoral. Posing as a prostitute falls so far outside the scope of respectability, it has always been a challenge to try to salvage anything useful from her story. Consequently, the verdict long ago for Tamar was a resounding "guilty as charged." It's hard to imagine any other interpretation of the facts. She is summarily upbraided in commentaries as a wicked woman, a vindictive schemer, a snare to Judah, and for her willingness to compromise anything, even her purity, just to have a baby. She's certainly no candidate for a role model. So for as long as anyone can remember, the case involving Tamar has been closed.

In recent years, however, scholars reviewing her file have discovered enough new evidence to warrant reopening the case. A bit of careful detective work reveals there may be more to Tamar's story than we first thought.

The first clue that something isn't right comes from overt statements made about Tamar in her story and elsewhere in Scripture that simply do not square with the original verdict. When Judah was exposed as the father of her unborn child, he said, "She is more *righteous* than I" (Genesis 38:26, emphasis added). Usually this is regarded as a confession of Judah's guilt, rather than an exoneration of Tamar. In gathering evidence for Tamar's case,

he thought Tamar was a hired prostitute

Judah's statement was thrown out as irrelevant, without anyone weighing what, if anything, he was trying to tell us about her. Now, however, Tamar's defense team would like the opportunity to cross-examine Judah to understand his meaning.

It seems strange, too, that later on, when Boaz (a man of impeccable character and a direct descendant of Judah) took Ruth to be his wife, the elders of Bethlehem honored their union with a heartfelt blessing for Boaz that ended, "May your family be like that of Perez, whom *Tamar* bore to Judah" (Ruth 4:12, emphasis added). If Tamar is some scandalous skeleton in the family closet, why would anyone bring her up on a holy occasion like this? One would think this was the height of bad taste and an embarrassment to the family. Yet Tamar is named without apology in a statement intended to honor the bride and groom.

Add to this the fact that just a few generations later, her name resurfaced twice when King David and his son Absalom both named their beautiful daughters after their great-great-grandmother Tamar (2 Samuel 13:1; 14:27), a fact all the more puzzling because back then a name was more than a label. It represented a person's character and destiny. According to Tamar's long-standing reputation as the scheming woman who entrapped Judah, this was like naming your adorable baby daughter "Jezebel."

The second clue involves Tamar's motive, which is slightly more complicated since it entails delving into the ancient patriarchal culture, into customs completely foreign to the modern American mind. A twenty-first-century Korean CEO dropped a hint of ancient values when he said, "After death, a tiger leaves its skin. A man leaves his name."[2] In our culture, a man's name survives through the corporate empire he builds or through some notable office or accomplishment that earns him a place in the history books. In ancient times, a man's name lived on through his sons, which explains why God's promise of descendants was so important to the childless Abraham, who was tottering on the brink of extinction. To die without a male descendant was to be erased from history.

A CALL TO SACRIFICE

The ancient world had an emergency plan to save a childless dead man from extinction. In Moses' day, it was formalized as the Levirate Law (*levir* is Latin for "a husband's brother"; cf. Deuteronomy 25:5–10). In Judah's era it appears already to have been an established custom. According to this ancient custom, if a man died without a child, his brother would marry and impregnate his widow. The son born from this union inherited the name and the estate of the deceased. The living brother who refused this duty fell under deep disgrace. The solution was complicated, for it obliged *both* the widow and the living brother to make costly sacrifices for the man who had died. His widow couldn't just move on and start a new life. She was honor bound to preserve her husband's name. The surviving brother faced a moral dilemma as simple math will show.

Tamar's case concerned three brothers, Judah's three sons: Er, Onan, and Shelah. According to ancient laws of inheritance, Judah would divide his estate into four equal parts. Tamar's husband Er, as the eldest son, would inherit a *double* portion. Two out of four slices of the family pie, or, in this case, half of Judah's estate would go to him. His two younger brothers would each receive a single slice, or one-fourth.

When Er died childless, the math changed for his two surviving brothers. Now the same pie was divided three ways, with Onan (now in the place of Judah's firstborn) getting *two-thirds* instead of his original one-fourth portion—more than even Er would have inherited had he lived. Any accountant would smile over that kind of growth in assets.

Family duty to produce an heir for his dead brother threatened to spoil everything for Onan, who now was positioned to enjoy the financial prospects and the heightened privileges of the eldest son. Talk about a conflict of interest! If Tamar became pregnant with a son, Onan would forfeit his preeminent place in the family. Tamar's son would become Judah's new number-one son in place of Er, and Onan would slide back to his former second-son position, watching his inheritance shrink into a measly one-quarter portion again. There was the added risk that Onan might never father a second son to perpetuate his own name. The stakes were high. It required extraordinary sacrifice that modern readers don't naturally appreciate, but God routinely calls his people to make sacrifices for one another. Sacrifice for the good of others comes with being his image bearer.

This family duty to produce an heir to preserve Er's name is essential to understanding Tamar's motive and is the key to solving the case. If investigators miss this one piece of evidence, Tamar's motives sink to desperation for a child or, worse, determination to get even with her father-in-law for deceiving her. Onan didn't have a chance to shirk his responsibility to Tamar because his father commanded him: "Lie with your brother's wife and fulfill your duty to her as a brother-in-law to produce offspring for your brother" (Genesis 38:8).

JUDAH IN DECLINE

The background to Tamar's story centers on what was happening with Judah, the alleged "victim" of her crime. Ordinarily, anyone who had been reading through the book of Genesis from start to finish would at this point be completely gripped by the story of Judah's half brother Joseph, who was their father Jacob's clear favorite. Judah and his brothers (in a jealous passion) kidnapped and sold Joseph as a slave. The guilt of this crime against their brother (a felony today) and the sounds of Joseph's desperate pleas for mercy haunted his brothers from that day forward (Genesis 42:21).

To the reader's annoyance, the Judah-Tamar episode interrupts this drama just as Joseph is chained and dragged off to

Egypt.[3] Like a soap opera scriptwriter, the narrator takes the reader to the cliffhanger of Joseph's abduction, then diverts the camera to a far less interesting subplot about Judah's family. But the Judah storyline is key, and the narrator skillfully weaves it into Joseph's story with powerful effect.

In contrast to the exemplary moral character that Joseph exhibits in faraway Egypt even though no one is watching him (Genesis 39), Judah is in a spiritual nosedive. The impact of Tamar's actions on Judah adds an unexpected twist to her case. For a man whose life is spinning out of control, colliding with Tamar is more like hitting a cement barricade than bumping into a willing cast member from *Sex and the City*.

REVISITING THE CRIME SCENE

"Judah got a wife for Er, his firstborn" (Genesis 38:6). The story of Tamar (presumably of Canaanite descent) starts here, with her marriage to Judah's eldest son. If they followed normal marriage customs, Tamar's father and father-in-law made the arrangements, most likely based on the political and financial advantages this union would bring to them.

However well this merger may have turned out for the two family heads, the marriage was a complete disaster for Tamar. Lots of couples talk about the struggles of that first year of marriage. Tamar's marriage was a nightmare by anyone's standard. Any girlhood hopes she may have had for her future life were quickly shattered by her new husband. Scripture tells us her new husband was "wicked in the Lord's sight," but spares us the gruesome details. No one spared Tamar, however. She lived with Er's wickedness every day. A dull, unhappy marriage is bad enough. Marriage to a *wicked* man is in a league all its own. Tamar's marriage to Er was the antithesis of the Blessed Alliance. No one knows what Tamar suffered, but suffer she did. Er's wickedness was so terrible, God stepped in and took his life. His story is a microcosm of Noah's day and of Sodom and Gomorrah, where God acted decisively in judgment against wickedness on the earth.

Any relief Tamar felt at the death of her husband was short-lived. With Er's death, she went from one crisis to another. In a brief span of time, her miserable marriage to Er was followed by a second marriage, to his brother Onan, who shared her responsibility to rescue the unworthy Er from extinction, but who turned out to be just as bad as his dead brother. Onan *pretended* to do the honorable thing by marrying Tamar and having sexual relations with her, but each time they were together, he "spilled his semen on the ground to keep from producing offspring for his brother" (Genesis 38:9). Apparently he repeatedly degraded her by using her for his pleasure, then denying her the opportunity to conceive. One can only imagine how appalling and humiliating his actions were for Tamar, all the more so since she had entered this second marriage for the sake of honor and family loyalty. To make matters worse, she was powerless to do anything about Onan's cover-up. But not everyone in this story was powerless.

Once again, God stepped in. "What [Onan] did was wicked in the LORD's sight" (Genesis 38:10). Ironically, Onan lost his life by trying to save it. Suddenly Judah was down to one living son, with growing suspicions that Tamar was the problem—a hazard to his sons. Fearful that marriage to Tamar would cost him his third son, Shelah, too, Judah stalled by sending his daughter-in-law back to her father's house to live as a widow until his youngest son was grown. Tamar complied, but still remained under Judah's authority and legally betrothed to Shelah.

She waited. A long time passed. Shelah grew to manhood, but Judah showed no sign of keeping his promise. Tamar knew her duty, but Judah was blocking her path. The disgrace of her child-lessness would be significantly worse if her husband's name was cut off. She had no legal recourse. No one spoke in her defense. Tamar was in an impossible predicament.

Once again convinced of Judah's intention (or lack of intention), a marked change came over her. Up to this point she had accepted a passive role. She was always the object of the action. Judah *got* her for Er, *gave* her to Onan, and *sent* her home to wait for Shelah. When she heard that Judah, just recovered from being widowed himself, was on his way to the shearing of his sheep, Tamar saw a window of opportunity that she would seize. Now the verbs belong to her. In a flurry of deliberate action, Tamar shed her widow's garments along with her passivity, veiled herself to play the prostitute and conceal her true identity, and placed herself in Judah's path. He has been without a wife for sometime now. Tamar will exploit his loneliness.

It's worth noting, at this point, that investigators of ancient history have uncovered ancient Hittite and Assyrian laws that regulated the levirate duty. These documents not only placed responsibility on the brother of the deceased but, interestingly enough, they also supported marriage of the father-in-law to his son's widow if no brother fulfilled this duty. Although biblical regulations later prohibit this, it seems plausible, especially in light of Tamar's conduct, that in Judah's day the father-in-law was responsible if his son failed to fulfill his duty. According to such laws, and also to the Bible's view of Tamar, conception by a father-in-law was a legitimate means of saving a family member from being cut off. Furthermore, now that Judah was a widow, no wrong would be done against his wife.

The whole episode gives terrible insight into Judah's character. What on earth made Tamar think such a scheme would work? Surely a godly man seeing a prostitute in his path would recoil and pass by on the other side of the road like the priest and the Levite in Jesus' parable of the Good Samaritan. Evidently Tamar knew Judah well enough to know her plan would succeed. She was not bringing him down. He was down already. He saw the prostitute, approached her, and the bargaining began.

Judah skipped the small talk and got straight to the point. "Come now, let me sleep with you" (Genesis 38:16). Tamar negotiated like a hardheaded businesswoman, first exacting payment, then letting him set the price. Clearly Judah was acting on impulse, for he did not have the goat he promised in payment for her services. He would deliver one later. She demanded a pledge and this time shrewdly set the terms herself: his seal and the staff in his hand. The seal was an engraved ring or cylinder made of stone or metal, which a man wore around his neck on a cord. He used it to emboss his insignia on legal documents. She wanted both the seal and the cord. The staff symbolized his authority and was carved with unique markings to indicate it belonged to Judah. By surrendering these articles, Judah demonstrated how intent (and reckless) he was in getting what he wanted. Tamar left the scene of the crime with the equivalent of Judah's ID: his credit card and driver's license. Now, even without the aid of DNA testing, Tamar can prove the identity of the father of her unborn child.

JUDAH'S SHOCKING VERDICT

If the double standard didn't exist already, it was born the second Judah learned his daughter-in-law was pregnant and guilty of prostitution. In an indignant outburst Judah condemned Tamar and sentenced her to die for a crime he knew lay in his own past. "Bring her out and have her burned to death!" (Genesis 38:24). How quick we are to cast the first stone when Jesus isn't standing there to look us in the eye. This certainly demonstrates the absolute power Judah had over Tamar, even while she was living with her father. Some wonder if Judah wasn't taking advantage of an opportunity to rid his family of his daughter-in-law. Regardless, this blackest of all moments in Judah's personal history will be shockingly brief, for Tamar is about to turn on the lights.

As they bring her out to face execution, she sends a message to her father-in-law with evidence that stops him cold. "I am pregnant by the man who owns these.... See if you recognize whose seal and cord and staff these are" (Genesis 38:25). Tamar's timing was perfect and precipitated one of the most dramatic moments in biblical history, not simply because of the shocking revelation but for something she never could have anticipated—her father-in-law's reaction.

This was a watershed moment for Judah, the eye-opening instant when the prodigal comes to his senses. Tamar's bold confrontation had the same effect on Judah as the words "You are the man!" had on David after his affair with Bathsheba (2 Samuel 12:7). King David broke in repentance. Something similar happened to Judah. Historically, Hebrew translators have worded Judah's response as a *relative* statement—"She is *more* righteous than I, since I wouldn't give her to my son Shelah" (Genesis 38:26, emphasis added). This has led interpreters to conclude that Judah was taking the "greater share" of the blame to himself, although they are quick to add that Tamar bore blame too.

Contemporary Old Testament scholars have come out with more precise translations in which Judah takes *full* blame and not only acquits his daughter-in-law of wrongdoing but actually *praises* her by saying, "She is righteous, not I"[4] or "She is in the right, not I."[5] This puts Tamar's actions in a different light and leaves Christians sputtering. How are we supposed to reconcile Judah's statement with what Tamar has done?

Judah's words blow holes in the theories that Tamar was simply trying to get even with him or was desperate for a child. Scripture clearly frowns on those who take vengeance into their own hands, instead of trusting God to settle old scores. Such a motive could hardly be called righteous. Besides, what would she accomplish if, in the end, Judah had the last word by sentencing her to die? As for having a child, how could Tamar possibly hope to recover her honor by becoming a mother if she threw away her reputation by resorting to prostitution? According to Judah, something deeper drove his daughter-in-law to such radical measures. He saw it right away and called her righteous.

A RIGHTEOUS WOMAN

The Bible doesn't carelessly throw around a word like "righteous." Righteousness belongs to God and is the comfort of his people. "The LORD is righteous in all his ways" (Psalm 145:17). It's reassuring to know—especially with so much wrong in the world—that there's a God in heaven who cares about justice and truth and who *always* does what is right. He sets the standard for what is right, and when his people bear his image, they do what is right too. No Old Testament person, especially someone from Judah's background, would ever thoughtlessly apply "righteous" to a Canaanite, like Tamar. The word simply means too much.

The prophet Habakkuk linked righteousness to faith in God. You can't have righteousness without also having God. Righteous living—doing the right thing in God's eyes no matter how much it costs you—is a sign that you belong to him. "The righteous will live by their faith" (Habakkuk 2:4 NLT).

The contrast between the righteous and the wicked runs like a major artery through the Scriptures. Throughout the Old Testament, righteousness distinguishes God's people from everyone else. They desire to do what pleases God. His righteousness is their compass in deciding their actions and making choices. Righteous living is a recurring theme in Proverbs—a *life-giving* approach to living, whereas wickedness destroys and kills. Even here, Tamar's righteous actions stand in sharp relief against the wickedness of Judah's sons. Judah couldn't have paid Tamar a higher compliment than to call her righteous. He was saying, "She has done the right thing. She has done what pleases God. And I have not."

Put more bluntly, Judah deliberately engaged in prostitution. Tamar fought for his family. As a descendant of Abraham and Sarah, Judah's impulsive actions profanely devalued and squandered the promised seed. Tamar regarded his seed as sacred and risked her life to preserve it. They are polarized in their objectives and their actions. He is seeking pleasure for himself. She is laying down her life for others. Judah spoke the truth. Tamar was righteous, and he was not.

The narrator validates Judah's surprising verdict. This family lives under the watchful eye of El Roi—the God who sees and cares. He calls them to walk in his ways and doesn't hide his disapproval of their actions when they don't. Twice the narrator states that what Judah's sons did was "wicked in the LORD's sight." Twice he tells us God acted decisively to stop their wickedness. What is more, the narrator records Judah's condemnation of himself when he confesses his wickedness before God. But there is no reproach for Tamar, no "What Tamar did was wicked in the LORD's sight." Instead, the heavens are strangely silent.

For generations, commentators have attempted to correct this oversight—qualifying Judah's words, highlighting Tamar's deception, condemning her actions, even defending Judah. None of this is in the text. According to the Bible, Tamar was righteous. She sided with God and did the right thing. Perhaps it is time we allowed the Bible's view of Tamar to stand.

THE RESCUE OF A MAN

In *Wild at Heart: Discovering the Secret of a Man's Soul*, John Eldredge describes a woman as a maiden waiting in a tower for a man to rescue her—a description that has troubled a lot of women. Tamar turns the tables. She is an *ezer*-warrior who rescues men. She carries out a stunning rescue of Judah's two dead sons with her twins, Perez and Zerah. She saves *both* Er and Onan from extinction, despite their wickedness.

But Tamar also rescued Judah. His collision with her brought a halt to his steep spiritual decline. Driven by rejection and jealous anger over his father's preference for Rachel over his mother Leah, and for favoring Rachel's sons, Joseph and Benjamin, over Judah and his brothers, Judah led the conspiracy against Joseph and instigated selling him as a slave. Now with Joseph off the scene, their elderly father Jacob doted protectively on Joseph's younger brother Benjamin. Hurt and fed up, Judah left his brothers and migrated into Canaanite territory. He lived among Canaanites, forged alliances with Canaanites, married a Canaanite, and ultimately started behaving like one. Instead of walking with God, he walked away. He seemed indifferent to his wicked sons and even barred Tamar's path to obedience. Judah was a strong, determined man, and *he* was lost. He met his match in Tamar.

God is, as we have said, in the business of changing lives, and Judah becomes a masterpiece. Judah's turning point came when he collided with Tamar. The evidence showed up later when Benjamin's life was threatened and Judah, a man once ruled by jealousy and resentment, volunteered to die in his half brother's place. This is not simply one man laying down his life for his beloved brother. This is the *rejected* son offering himself in place of his father's pet. Clearly Judah had become a righteous man.

But even Tamar would not live to see the full impact of her efforts. As the descendants of Abraham mushroomed into a nation, the blood line of her eldest son, Perez, became the golden cord that connected God's promise of a redeemer in Eden with the birth of Jesus in Bethlehem thousands of years later. The crowning glory of Tamar's efforts came when the name *Jesus* was inscribed on the Perez branch of Judah's family tree.

RECOVERING A RIGHTEOUS ROLE MODEL

Tamar didn't corrupt the line of Christ. She rescued it! She and the other three women in Matthew's genealogy were kingdom builders, not destroyers. Furthermore, Tamar adds an interesting and vitally needed piece to our discussion of what it means to be a woman. For generations we have successfully kept Tamar out of this conversation, and that choice has been costly—for women and for men. Judah lifted the ban on Tamar by calling her righteous. We can't understand our calling as women, and we'll never make sense of relationships between men and women, until Tamar takes part in shaping our conclusions.

In church, we talk about the importance of a "quiet and gentle spirit" (1 Peter 3:4) as though the Bible has nothing else to say about women, doesn't also require these qualities in godly men,[6] and doesn't equally prize a woman's strength. Tamar sets us straight. She wasn't called righteous for her quiet and gentle spirit. She was righteous by being strong and assertive. She was a godly leader. She confronted Judah, the future leader of Jacob's family, for turning his back on God's covenant, and her courageous actions led him back to God. She was committed to build the house of Jacob and used her strength, her wit, and her courage to do what was right in God's eyes. Judah rightly called her righteous.

Dropping a strong woman like Tamar from the lineup of biblical female role models confuses women into thinking it's okay to turn a blind eye instead of speaking up when sin is in the family or the church. It also causes a lot of godly women to feel that their strength is all wrong. To be sure, strength, like any other gift, can be misused by a man or a woman. But righteous strength like Tamar's is an asset to the church. When we discard the strength of women, we disable a powerful weapon against the Enemy and remove a vital safeguard for men. God calls the *ezer* to be strong.

Tamar puts starch back into our definition of what it means to be a woman. She would have loved Paul's letter to the Ephesians. He was speaking her language when he urged believers to "be strong in the Lord" and to arm themselves as warriors ready to "stand against the devil's schemes" (Ephesians 6:10–18).

Women are okay with this kind of language in some settings and actually fight a lot of righteous battles. We're highly visible in the PTA, Mothers Against Drunk Drivers, and all sorts of political campaigns and social organizations. We're fearless when fighting for our kids, building relationships, and improving our careers. In the church, we're unstoppable when it comes to developing and advancing women's and children's ministries. Our boldness wanes when it comes to the men in our lives, but that's where Tamar takes us. She wasn't fighting for her rights, nor was she at war with Judah. Her battle was for God's purposes, and she didn't hold back. For Judah's sake alone, it was a good thing that she didn't.

Tamar is the best role model in Genesis for the *ezer*, the strong helper. She is rightly included in Matthew's genealogy as a forerunner of the king. She expands the range of the *ezer*'s influence beyond hearth and home to encompass her father-in-law and God's covenant with his people. Although her tactics wouldn't work today, the principles she represents do. Women are called to think about where men are leading, to stand against wrong, and to be leaders for God's purposes.

Tamar shatters the traditional definition of what it means to be a woman by standing up to the most powerful man in her life—her father-in-law and the tribal patriarch. For a time, she takes the symbols of authority away from the man who tells her whom to marry and where to live—a man who can sentence her to death without answering to anyone. Before returning the articles Judah had given her, she pointed Judah back to the God of the covenant, the only true authority over both of their lives. And what impact did her actions have on him?

Judah gave Tamar the highest marks for her conduct and accepted her righteous rebuke. Her actions didn't emasculate or feminize him, as we are warned will happen if a woman takes the initiative. She didn't rob Judah of his manhood. To the contrary, he became a *better* man because of his encounter with her. One wonders what would have become of Judah if Tamar had held her peace and remained passive. The strength of a woman is a powerful weapon for rescue, healing, and peace when women like Tamar are "strong in the Lord."

Tamar concludes our study of the women in Genesis and expands our understanding of the *ezer*. The next woman, Hannah, is one of the most beloved figures in Scripture. She was a mother with a heart for God, but we will soon learn the small domestic battle this *ezer* was fighting would have repercussions even she couldn't have anticipated.

FOCUS: Negative views of Tamar don't square with the high honor biblical writers consistently accord her whenever they mention her name. We want to rehabilitate Tamar as a strong role model for women and explore the significance of her righteous example for us today.

TAMAR'S STORY: Genesis 38; Ruth 4:12; Matthew 1:3

FOR DISCUSSION, READ: Genesis 38

1. How have we lost Tamar? What usually comes to mind when we think of her?

2. Why is it important to reopen her case? What clues does the Bible leave for us that cause us to rethink our views of her?

3. What responsibility did Tamar share with her brothers-in-law?

4. Contrast Tamar's motives with the motives of Onan and Judah in avoiding this duty.

5. How is Tamar a strong example of an *ezer* in her relationships with the men in her story?

6. How did Tamar reflect God's image? And how did her bold actions change Judah's life?

7. Have you ever been "set straight" or rescued by someone you thought was "less righteous" than you? Explain.

8. Why is righteous Tamar such a powerful example for women today? How can we live for righteousness in our relationships and circumstances?

THE POWER BEHIND THE THRONE—

Hannah

She was lost in the travails of life, until she discovered her true mission as a mother.

Sonya was a child of adversity. This African-American woman (number twenty-two in a family of twenty-four children) spent most of her childhood in foster care and completed only a third-grade education. At thirteen she married an older man in hopes of escaping poverty. Instead of making good on his promises of a better life, he turned out to be a bigamist. When the marriage ended, her circumstances were worse than ever. She was uneducated, poor, living in a "cracker-box" house she couldn't afford, with two active boys to raise alone and no marketable skills to help her survive. But she was an *ezer*, and she declared war on the downward pull that threatened to sentence her sons to a life of poverty. Her only resources were her own two hands, a fierce determination to do whatever it took to make a better life for her sons, and her unbending faith in God.

She turned her resolve into action. She took jobs as a household domestic to pay the bills and implemented an ambitious agenda for her sons. She turned off the television, enforced a rigorous reading program that opened up new worlds for her boys, and never let them off the hook when it came to doing their homework. No one could have guessed—least of all Sonya—that through all her sufferings God was preparing her to raise one of the world's finest neurosurgeons and a bright light for the gospel of Jesus Christ. Her son, Dr. Ben Carson, now a nationally recognized figure and the director of pediatric neurosurgery at Johns Hopkins Hospital, openly acknowledges his indebtedness to his mother. In his own words, "I not only saw and felt the difference my mother made in my life, I am still living out that difference as a man."[1]

Back when the nation Israel was heading for a seismic shift in government—from the rule of judges to the rule of kings—God raised up another young woman for a mission greater than she could have imagined. Hannah's story, unlike Sonya's, had a more promising beginning. While we know nothing about her early life or how her marriage came about, we can be fairly sure her marriage with Elkanah was arranged according to the customs of the day. The outcome was to this bride's advantage, for she ended up with a man who adored her. In a culture that valued women primarily for their ability to reproduce, Elkanah was a welcome exception. He loved Hannah simply for herself, with a love that was "as strong as death" and as "unyielding as the grave" (Song of Songs 8:6). Nothing could diminish it. Not even the fact that she failed him where he needed her most.

SLIDING INTO SECOND

Hannah's story begins by spotlighting the family tree of her husband. Elkanah was the fifth generation of a strong family that was counting on Hannah to deliver the sixth by presenting her husband with a son. Then we read the killer lines that pull us into the story as compellingly as any suspense novel. "[Elkanah] had *two* wives; one was called Hannah and the other Peninnah. Peninnah had children, but Hannah had none" (1 Samuel 1:2, emphasis added). In two brief sentences, we are introduced to the sorrow that defined Hannah's life. Hannah was infertile—a miserable fact made a hundred times worse by the fact that Peninnah, the "other woman" in the family, was making up for Hannah's shortcomings by bearing children to Elkanah, both sons and daughters.

The evils of polygamy against women are nowhere more apparent than in the Elkanah household. Both wives were tormented—the one because she was infertile, the other because she was unloved. It was a recipe for disaster. Within the ancient culture, a husband in Elkanah's circumstances was well within the boundaries of respectability in adding another wife. As noted previously, a man had to have a son. His honor, his name, and his family's survival depended on it. No matter how much he loved Hannah, her feelings were secondary to the all-consuming goal of producing sons. Even today, in some Third World countries where patriarchal values prevail, a man will divorce a barren wife or one who conceives only daughters and start over with a different woman.

Peninnah rescued the family line with her repeated success in bearing children, but at the same time became a bitter intrusion into what might have been one of the Bible's greatest love stories. With the birth of Peninnah's first son, her value soared while Hannah's standing in the community plummeted. Hannah may have been first in Elkanah's heart, but Peninnah was unquestionably first in the eyes of the community. Not only did Hannah suffer the indignity of sharing her husband with another woman, she had to live in the shadow of Peninnah's repeated triumphs in childbearing. Sadly, this was only the beginning of Hannah's sufferings.

SWALLOWED BY SUFFERING

Women who suffer from infertility know what an emotional roller coaster it is with monthly disappointments and the loud ticking of the biological clock. There's no escaping the sudden pang that comes when a friend announces she is pregnant or a baby shower invitation arrives in the mail. Little things can set you off and bring a rush of sorrow to the surface. One woman burst into tears in the cereal aisle of the grocery story after seeing several mothers with their babies. Mother's Day always proved the undoing of a cancer survivor friend of mine whose hopes of bearing children were permanently dashed by chemotherapy. She battled back tears in church as motherhood was celebrated and mothers around her were honored with roses. When the congregation rose to sing songs of praise to God for his goodness, her joyful voice was silent. "The words just stuck in my throat," she said.

Hannah experienced the normal sorrows of empty arms. But her ordeal was intensified—deliberately by Peninnah's mocking words and, inadvertently, by Elkanah, who, despite his great devotion to her, no longer shared her struggle.

Hannah's torment peaked on the family's annual pilgrimage to Shiloh, where they went to offer sacrifices and celebrate God's goodness. Each year on the road to worship—a public parade of Hannah's failure to conceive—Peninnah escalated her taunts. Surrounded by her lively brood, she smugly made the most of her superiority over Hannah.

The harassment went well beyond mere insensitivity. Peninnah's jabs were aimed directly at Hannah's faith in God, giving early hints that these domestic, small-scale tensions in Elkanah's family were actually part of a wider cosmic battle. The Hebrew language describing Peninnah's conduct links her to the enemies of God's people who taunted them with sneers of "Where is your God?"[2] Peninnah's cutting remarks suggested God was playing favorites and loved her more than Hannah. The painful implication was that Hannah was wasting her time to trust in God.

Elkanah unwittingly contributed to Hannah's sufferings too. His undying love didn't shield her from the anguish of abandonment. He not only abandoned her physically by dividing himself between her and Peninnah, he abandoned her emotionally as well. Instead of sharing her sufferings, he addressed the problem of infertility for himself through a second marriage and left Hannah to suffer alone. Elkanah was a complicated man. He embraced his culture's values in his determined quest for a son, yet defied those same values by his love and respect for Hannah even though she failed in her duty to bear children. Out of love, he gave her the double portion of food at the annual feast, which rightfully belonged to Peninnah or her firstborn son.

Later, when she makes a radical vow, he displays enormous respect for Hannah by refusing to veto her commitment, which was his legal prerogative as a husband (Numbers 30:10–15).[3]

Signs of spousal abandonment appeared when Hannah, worn down from Peninnah's verbal abuse en route to Shiloh, wept and refused to eat. Under the circumstances, who of us wouldn't push her dinner away? Depression takes the flavor out of everything. Hannah's despondency and loss of appetite threatened to put a damper on the family feast. Elkanah thought his love should make up the difference and dispel her depression. After all, he reasoned, "You have me—isn't that better than having ten sons?" (1 Samuel 1:8 NLT).

His unfeeling comment reminded her of the painful fact that she didn't have any sons and underscored the distance that had come between them. Instead of affirming and entering into her struggle, Elkanah simply pointed out to Hannah why she shouldn't feel depressed. His "look on the bright side" approach simply heaped more pain on one who was already collapsing under the weight of sorrow. So far as Elkanah was concerned, the crisis was over. He had children. For him, barrenness was a thing of the past. He had moved on. He wanted her to move on too. He was oblivious to the fact that the most important thing going on in his home at that particular moment (indeed, in the entire nation, as we will see) was his wife's infertility.

What in the world was God doing?

Family dynamics were only minor irritants to Hannah compared to the overriding reality that the Lord had kept her from bearing children. Twice (no doubt to make sure we get the message) the narrator states the fact that "*the* LORD had closed her womb" (1 Samuel 1:5–6, emphasis added). This bitter piece of information forms the centerpiece of Hannah's story. Hateful as Peninnah was and as insensitive as Elkanah could be, the real issue confronting Hannah was the abandonment by God. Maybe Peninnah was right. Maybe God *did* love her more than he loved Hannah. This certainly explains why Peninnah's ridicule was so potent. Hannah trusted God, and the bitter payoff was barrenness.

This is the part of the story that makes the sufferings of any child of God more difficult to bear. We assume we have the insider's advantage if we follow God's rules and always color inside the lines. We are taught that God cares especially for us. So why do things only seem to get worse? All our prayers and pleadings seem to fall on deaf ears—and someone else, maybe someone who shows less interest in God, is sending out the birth announcements. Peninnah might provoke, and from time to time the well-meaning Elkanah might be insensitive. But ultimately Hannah's biggest struggle was with God—the God who had closed her womb, to whom she cried out countless times, all seemingly in vain. From Hannah's perspective, God was too busy doing good things for Peninnah and Elkanah to remember her. Hannah was as yet unaware of how much God was doing in the silence.

When I was a student at Westmont College, I took a detour after botany class one afternoon to wander through the lush gardens behind Kerrwood Hall, a former estate in the foothills of

Santa Barbara overlooking the Pacific Ocean. Most people who have visited there will tell you it is the next best thing to Paradise. After what I'd just heard in class about all of the chemical processes going on inside plants, the stillness of the garden seemed like a contradiction. I was sure that if everything that was happening in that garden made a noise, the sound of it would be deafening.

God's silence is not an accurate way to measure what he is doing. It's easy to forget he often does his best work when, so far as we can tell, he doesn't seem to be doing anything at all. But looking back on those long agonizing stretches of God's silence, most of us will say those were the times in our relationship with God when he was doing the most. In Hannah's case, although there was no physical evidence of his activity—no thunderbolt, no voice from heaven, no positive pregnancy test—God was doing a mighty work in Hannah's heart.

The first sign of God's activity in Hannah's life was not, as we might expect, when Hannah discovered she was pregnant at last with Samuel. The first sign came when, exhausted from Peninnah's ridicule and broken by her childlessness, Hannah dropped to her knees in Shiloh and poured out her heart to God in prayer. I can understand why Hannah lost her appetite and pushed her dinner away. What I find hard to explain is why she didn't push God away too. Yet the endless suffering, which threatened to destroy her faith in God, actually served the opposite purpose of driving her to him in remarkably relentless faith. The Hannah who weeps and prays is anything but hard and cold toward God. It is a powerful sign that God is active in Hannah—the first great reversal in her story.

Hannah aches. She weeps and prays. She implores the Lord to look on her misery and to remember her. Fervently she prays for a son. Although Hannah feels that God may have abandoned her, her prayer indicates she has not abandoned God. We all wince (then conveniently forget) when she vows to give back the son she yearns for more than life itself. We'll think about that some other time. For now we, along with Eli the priest who is watching her as she prays, are more taken by her desperation. Hannah was so caught up in her anguish and her pursuit of God, she may have been praying openly the way a lot of us pray in private when our struggles get the best of us—when we let ourselves go and our weeping and crying out to God are unrestrained by any awareness of onlookers. Hannah's prayer is so impassioned, we are moved with pity. Eli thought she was drunk and rebuked her. His mix-up is an indictment of the spiritual state of things in the tabernacle as well as in the nation. Israel's leadership seems sadly unacquainted with such heartfelt praying. After hearing her explanation, a befuddled Eli readjusts his spiritual spectacles along with his faulty assessment of her and lends his blessing to her prayer. "Go in peace, and may the God of Israel grant you what you have asked of him" (1 Samuel 1:17).

Now her story accelerates and brings us to the second reversal, where God ends Hannah's barrenness. After returning to Ramah, "Elkanah lay with Hannah his wife, and the Lord remembered her" (1 Samuel 1:19). At long last, the God who closed Hannah's womb blessed her with the conception of new life. Hannah gave birth to the child for whom she had longed and prayed, and Peninnah's awful taunts faded into silence. After Samuel's birth, Hannah suspended her trips to Shiloh until after she had weaned her child and could take him to the tabernacle as she had promised. (In biblical times, a child could be weaned as late as three or perhaps even four years old,) which is only slightly comforting. Samuel may not have been a toddler when she left him at the tabernacle, but he was still unbearably young to be separated from his mother.

Nevertheless, Hannah kept her word. She took her little son to Shiloh, where she led him in sacrifice and worship. Samuel heard his mother pray with words that rival the best of David's psalms—words that stayed with him for the rest of his life. And then she left him there, under the care and tutelage of Eli the priest and in the company of Eli's two sons, whom we learn in the very next sentence "were wicked men" (1 Samuel 2:12). Samuel's new environment was hair-raising from any mother's perspective. Yet Hannah fulfilled her vow and entrusted her little son to God. Although it's difficult for us to fathom how she did it, Hannah returned home to Ramah, childless once again, but this time with a heart at rest and (one would hope) a speechless Peninnah.

UNDERSTANDING HANNAH

When my daughter was eighteen months old, the mother of a college freshman told me she felt teary and depressed for weeks after her daughter left for college. At the time, the emotional crisis she suffered seemed a little excessive to me. Now as my eighteen-year-old daughter is packing for her launch, the "excessive" emotions of that mother make a lot more sense to me.

I know Hannah is widely regarded as a role model because of her prayer life. But as a mother, I find it hard to relate to Hannah's style of praying. I find the content of Hannah's two surviving prayers disturbing. First she prays for a child. I understand that part. But then in the same breath she vows to give him up, which makes no sense to the mother in me. Then, when the wrenching moment comes to part with him, instead of sobbing and falling apart as we might expect, given what happened the last time she prayed at the tabernacle, Hannah is remarkably composed. She prays a lengthy prayer that appears completely unrelated to the searing separation that is just moments away. None of the "Lord help Samuel be a good boy, protect him, guard his heart, help him be brave" (interspersed with sobs) kind of prayer we'd pray if we were in Hannah's shoes.

Instead, Hannah is triumphant. She radiates joy. This is the day of Hannah's strength. Considering the circumstances, her words are baffling. "My heart rejoices in the LORD; in the LORD my [strength] is lifted high" (1 Samuel 2:1). With her little child nestled close against her side and their hearts about to be torn in two, Hannah continues with lofty words that send the mind soaring with a glorious vision of God. "Launched by intensely personal experience—*my* heart, *my* strength, *my* God, *my* mouth, *my* enemies, *my* victory—[Hannah's] prayer is soon in orbit around God.... To our great surprise we hear Hannah singing and praying not about her precious pregnancy and lovely child, but about her incomparable God and God's incredible ways."[4] How are we to make sense of this?

We will never understand Hannah until we begin with the assumption that her heart beats the same as ours do, that she has feelings just like we do. In her barrenness she was, by her own admission, in bitterness of soul. She wanted nothing more in all of life than to hold a baby of her own. Only when we allow these very human passions to exist in Hannah will we begin to see the fierceness of her love for God. Yes, she languished in her longings for a child. Yes, she was devastated when her husband took a second wife. Yes, she felt every sting of Peninnah's barbs. And yes, she prayed relentlessly that God would give her a child. But somewhere along the line everything changed for Hannah and something else became even more important. That change showed up when Hannah prayed.

Hannah's psalms[5] seem to reveal that everything changed for her when she realized Peninnah was laughing at God. Suddenly, much as Hannah longed for a child, she wanted something else even more. She wanted God to vindicate himself as the God who hears and answers the prayers of those who trust in him. In prayer, she raised her sword in the battle for God's glory. The passion of her heart voiced the passion of the prayer Jesus later taught his disciples— "Hallowed be your name" (Matthew 6:9). She willingly offered up her most priceless treasure to shut the mouth of the one who dared to mock her God. Hannah was an *ezer*. She subdued and ruled over God's enemies. She sacrificed for his glory. She stood squarely in the path of those who mocked him and fought to take back the honor and praise that rightfully belonged to him. And so she offered up Samuel, before he was even conceived.

Our love of happy endings is relentless. One of my friends suffered a prolonged ordeal with infertility, then tragically lost her baby when he was a toddler. People are always wanting to know, "Did she have any more children?" as though that could ever bring an end to the pain of her loss. In Hannah's case, we console ourselves with the fact that after Samuel, God gave her five more children—three sons and two daughters. According to our calculations, God amply compensated Hannah for her costly sacrifice. She gave up one child, gave birth to five more: one to make up for the loss of Samuel and four more to spare. Simple math tells us she came out ahead by four. Our calculations are all wrong.

Hannah always felt the enormity of her sacrifice, as any mother would. My grandmother lost a child shortly after his birth. Even though she had four living children and ended up with a slew of grandchildren, when she was old and gray, he was still on her mind, and she spoke wistfully of John Clark. There is no describing the emptiness Hannah felt when she returned home, a place no longer ringing with the laughter and shouts of her little boy at play. And what of those long quiet evenings with no child to tuck in for the night? He was so far away. No telephone, no email, no way to stay in touch. No little face gazing up at her as she dressed or fed or cuddled him. No small hand in hers. No mathematical equation could even out Hannah's sacrifice. Her separation from Samuel left a permanent hole in her heart. So what explains her joy?

THE POWER OF A MOTHER'S THEOLOGY

The first time I heard Joni Eareckson Tada speak, her message was unexpectedly powerful. Although several thousand people were in the audience, you could have heard a pin drop. By the time Joni finished, our hearts were turned to God and there wasn't a dry eye in the place. The power of the message was in the truth Joni spoke about the faithfulness of God and of the wisdom of trusting him, no matter what. But the impact of her message was more potent because her words—which were both personal and profoundly theological—were framed in her long history of paralysis. Pain, suffering, and frailty remained in her body, yet she radiated joy and strength.

When Hannah took a very young Samuel to Shiloh and knelt with him in worship before leaving him behind to serve the Lord all the days of his life, the frame around her words was her long history of infertility and persecution for her faith in God. Hannah knelt in prayer that day within the context of a relationship with God that had withstood the tests of time and of adversity. As I think of her, I am struck again by her remarkable composure as she took her son through what had to be the most difficult day of her life. The secret of Hannah's state of mind resides in the words she is praying, for Hannah's heart is fixed on her great God. She had walked with him down a long and bitter road and *because of her suffering* had come to know him better. Her prayer is like a page out of her private journal, where we enter Hannah's interior world and see her heart for God. He brought her to the end of herself so that she could go deeper with him.

The frame surrounding Hannah's prayer heightens the impact of her words *on herself* at that particularly difficult moment and *on us* in the difficulties we are facing today. Hannah's feet were on a rock because her trust was in God. Her heart, though doubled up with pain at the prospect of parting with Samuel, was nevertheless at peace and overflowed with praise and thanksgiving. God was on her mind, and she spoke only of him. As

Eugene Peterson says, "God's people fall to their knees in a pool of light."[6] The light that shone on Hannah as she prayed was the truth she learned about God through her barrenness.

Professional theologians continue to probe and ponder the rich theology that floods her prayer. I find myself going back to her words, again and again, in search of the source of Hannah's peace and joy. Always she points me to God. She lived in a world that was just as uncertain and frightening as the one we know. Righteousness was in decline, and if Eli's sons were any indicator (which they were), wickedness was on the rise. The nation was entering a tumultuous phase as God's people transitioned from the judges to the kings. From that day on Hannah was severed from the child she had longed for and loved with every fiber of her being. And, at the end of the day, she would go home with Elkanah and Peninnah—the same two people who had broken her heart a hundred times before by their choices and actions. Yet despite all of this, Hannah was secure and uncharacteristically confident, for she had come to understand that God is on his throne, and the one who trusts in him, though she is hurting, is standing on solid rock.

As she prays, Hannah spreads before every woman, every mother, every man, a breathtaking view of God's vast and sweeping rule over life and death and everything between. "The LORD brings death and makes alive; he brings down to the grave and raises up" (1 Samuel 2:6). His reign ranges from the secrets of the human body to the public rise and fall of political leaders and nations. Even the great reversals of life, those changes we seek and the ones we fear—wealth and poverty, health and sickness, conception and barrenness—are in his hands. Things done covertly, by plot, subversion, power, or deadly force, as well as things that happen by accident are all under his thumb. (They must serve his good purposes for us, no matter what someone else intends. Truly Hannah's theology is good news we desperately need when we pick up a newspaper or the phone rings in the middle of the night. Her words reassured a mother of teenagers, who in her forties was shocked to find she was pregnant and about to start all over again. Hannah the _ezer_ lived in a world where God is Lord over all. Nothing—not even a foe like Peninnah—stands beyond the reach of his reign.

Hannah was a realist too. After what she had been through and what she was facing, she was under no illusion that because she was God's child she would be spared the painful side of life. Like the rest of us, she still had to contend with the fact that suffering knocked her off her feet. Even the strongest among us will falter against the blast of the winds and the waves. Doubt, fear, and depression assault us all, no matter how much theology we've mastered. Hannah tells us by her life, as well as by her words, that the struggles that humble us are important regardless of the outcome. God uses the hard places of life to make us strong. By her own account, "those who stumbled are armed with strength" (1 Samuel 2:4). Hannah was strong _because_ she had stumbled and fallen flat on her face.

So what of those desperate moments when we've had enough—when the pressures are too much, and we can't take any more—and something bad happens anyway, and we fear we'll lose our faith. How can God do this to me? Reading between the lines of Hannah's psalm tells us just how close to the edge she had come. Evidently she had moments when she wondered if her faith would last. That's how Hannah discovered that God will "guard the feet of his saints" (1 Samuel 2:9). How else are we to explain why, when the combined forces of prolonged infertility, Peninnah's abuse, and God's silence pushed her to the edge of a spiritual cliff, she turned to God instead of turning away. Hannah wasn't holding onto God so much as he was holding onto her. He was guarding her feet, gripping her by the ankles. Her feet would not slip. He kept her from falling over the edge.

God isn't the only one who listens to our prayers. Prayer is a way of talking to ourselves. Hannah used prayer to good effect.

Amen
Do not forget the Verse

She was talking to God while at the same time telling herself the truth about him. Her words had the same reassuring effect on her that a hospital patient discovers, in those apprehensive hours before surgery, as she reflects on the surgeon's superb reputation and skill. By giving thanks to God, Hannah reminded herself that God was in control over the events that were breaking her heart, that he was at work in her pain to draw her closer and make her strong, and that he was holding her tightly and was not about to let her go. No one would have guessed—least of all Hannah—that through all her sufferings God was preparing her to raise one of Israel's godliest leaders, the mentor of the nation's first kings, or that so much could be done in so little time.

Hannah's child was also listening to her prayer. The whole time she was speaking, close by her side—so close she could feel the warmth of his small body—was her young son, Samuel, listening to every word. Ancient society defined a successful mother as a woman who presented her husband with sons. Our culture defines successful mothers in terms of the economic, social, and career success of her children. God calls mothers to a higher mission. His calling for Hannah and for Sonya Carson entailed raising their sons to be warrior image bearers for God's kingdom—a calling no less binding on mothers of daughters. Hannah and Sonya Carson pointed their children to God and raised them to live for him. However we define motherhood today, we must factor Hannah into our thinking as a major role model.

Hannah's sufferings equipped her for a vital mission. What she learned about God through her infertility helped her to equip her son for any contingency in life. The theology of Samuel's mother lodged in Samuel's young heart and prepared him for the road ahead. Later, as an adult, Samuel could easily have spoken the words of Sonya Carson's illustrious son, "I not only saw and felt the difference my mother made in my life, I am still living out that difference as a man."[7] But the impact of Hannah's theology didn't stop with Samuel.

THE HAND THAT ROCKS THE CRADLE

To get the full impact of Hannah's life we have to step back and view her in the flow of Israel's history. Then some rather startling details about her significance come to light. As we've already noted, she arrived on the scene when the nation was transitioning from the period of the judges to the rule of the kings. Spiritually, the nation was adrift. The people were indifferent to God. The priesthood was hopelessly corrupt.

Suddenly the flow of biblical history narrows its focus to one woman's private life. Some have explained Hannah's role as "a fitting introduction" to a major leader like Samuel. A miraculous birth narrative was an appropriate way to signal a major change in leadership for Israel. But Hannah's contributions and her significance in Israel's history go well beyond simply giving birth, and it is a proper tribute for Hannah to be the lead story in the two-volume history named for her son.[8] As Peterson explains,

> The story of Hannah is a story in its own right. Hannah is not merely the mother of Samuel, the occasion of a birth story that functions as a kind of entry way to the dominating stories of Samuel, Saul, and David. She holds her own with the best of them. She is as significant, both historically and spiritually, as the three men who follow her in the Samuel narrative.[9]

Hannah emerges as a spiritual leader when this caliber of godly leadership was so lacking in the nation. She became a major theological influence and a shaper of the nation's character, and all as a result of the theology she learned when the Lord closed her womb.

Hannah passed her theology on to her son Samuel. Her teachings "will crown [his life] with grace and clothe [him] with honor" (Proverbs 1:9 NLT). The same theology that held her through her barrenness, guided and fortified Samuel to walk with God during a perilous time for the nation — through the rise and fall of Eli and his wicked sons, of King Saul, and of the great King David.

Hannah's teachings sustained Samuel through the awful pain of Israel's rejection of him in their demand for a king.

Samuel took his mother's theology into Israel's throne room. He mentored Israel's first kings with the theology his mother learned in her longings for a child. Like matching bookends, Hannah's psalm inaugurates the age of Israel's monarchs, and the psalm of the elderly King David brings closure to the monarchy's opening scenes. David's psalm contains strong elements of Hannah's theology, which by then had entered into the heart of the king[10] and set the tone for the rule of Israel's kings. In the minds of some of the best Old Testament scholars, Hannah was the theologian of the monarchy, for her theology spelled out what was to come. At this perilous moment in Israel's history, God's purposes moved forward through a mother who struggled to understand the God who closed her womb. One wonders what would have become of Israel if not for Hannah.

MOTHERS AND WOMEN WHO LOVE KIDS

Things haven't changed much since Hannah's day. Life remains unpredictable, and we all have our ups and downs. We still struggle to understand the God who holds our lives in his hands and who at times withholds the blessings we crave. Women — moms, grandmothers, mentors, and friends — still pray and contend for the souls of the next generation and still, no doubt, underestimate the enormity of their influence on these young lives. While I was writing this chapter, five women contacted me by phone or email with reports of kids teetering on the edge. They were all praying and thinking of ways to love, connect, influence, and point these kids to Christ. These *ezers* are fighting battles, being brought low, refusing to hold back, and trusting God to work in the hearts of the young ones who are so dear to them.

I love the way C. S. Lewis characterized his wife after her death. Lewis was comforted to remember that his wife was in

God's hand—not merely in his care, but as a gleaming bright sword that he wields for the sake of his kingdom.

> "She is in God's hand." That gains a new energy when I think of her as a sword. Perhaps the earthly life I shared with her was only part of the tempering. Now perhaps He grasps the hilt; weighs the new weapon; makes lightnings with it in the air. "A right Jerusalem blade."[11]

It seems a fitting way to think of mothers like Hannah or Sonya or any other woman who throws in her lot with God and fights for a new generation of kingdom warriors. Hannah proves the *ezer*-warrior is a force to be reckoned with when she herself is a sword in God's hand. The spirit of Hannah lives on in us when we courageously fight for the lives God entrusts to us and point them to the God who is worthy of their trust.

Queen Esther, whose story is in the next chapter, was a sword in God's hand too, although she is more often remembered for her looks. To tell the truth, she probably would have been the last person to think of herself as a sword. Yet God called her to fight a battle that put her on the front lines of human history. Her story takes us directly to the apex of ancient world power, where men rule and vie for power, and women live to please.

FOCUS: For years Hannah was obsessed with her longings for a child. Through her struggle, she awakened to a deeper longing inside—the longing for God's glory. She was a true kingdom builder. We learn from Hannah how God uses struggle to reveal more of himself to us and to enlist us in his cause.

HANNAH'S STORY: 1 Samuel 1:1–28; 2:1–12, 18–21

FOR DISCUSSION, READ: 1 Samuel 1:1–20; 2:1–3, 9

1. Describe a personal longing you have had for something right and good that became the main focus in your relationship with God. How did it affect your relationship with him when he did not grant your request?

2. What was Hannah's main focus in her relationship with God?

3. How did the words and actions of Elkanah and Peninnah intensify her pain?

4. Can you relate to Hannah's desperation? Explain.

5. Discuss the turnaround in Hannah's attitude that led her from desperation to have a child to her willingness to give her child to God? What drove Hannah to make such a sacrifice?

6. What did Hannah learn about God that helps us understand the way he works in the world and in our personal lives?

7. How does it comfort us to know that God grips our feet?

8. What have you learned about God during times of struggle, and how does knowing him strengthen your passion to fill the earth with his glory?

Esther — A Sleeping Beauty

Being beautiful was her business, her art, her delight, and it took her a long way and earned her many dividends."

But her beauty didn't last. Beauty never does. As age lines appeared around this woman's eyes and her fair looks began to fade, the warm admiring spotlight that had become as comfortable as her own skin lost interest and drifted away. Heads stopped turning when she entered a room. Now younger beauties were receiving all the attention. That's when she got lost. As author Fredrick Buechner recalled his once strikingly beautiful mother, he reflected sadly that when she lost her beauty "she was like a millionaire who runs out of money.... she felt she had nothing left to offer the world.... So what she did was simply to check out of the world—that old, last rose of summer—the way Greta Garbo and Marlene Dietrich checked out of it, holing themselves up somewhere and never venturing forth except in disguise."[1]

At the other end of the spectrum, a thin young girl gazed in the mirror, not to ask, "Who is the fairest in the land," but to check whether she looked as fat today as she did yesterday. In a hushed whisper she admitted she was on the recovery side of an eating disorder, but that food continued to torture her. "I never stop thinking about food. There's no way to get away from it." In a world dominated by Madison Avenue, where the media daily bombard us with airbrushed images of physical perfection, it's easy to get duped into thinking you have nothing to offer the world—or a man—if you aren't blessed with a beautiful face and figure.

Esther's claim to fame was her beauty and her ability to please. It was a winning combination that took her a long way and put her name in lights. Even a book of the Bible bears her name. If she were alive today, she'd be featured on covers of fashion magazines and hounded by the paparazzi whenever she stepped out. Her face and form would define the standard for plastic surgery patients. Her hair and clothing would set fashion trends.

The ancient culture where she lived, like a lot of times and places in the world (most of them, to be honest), was a place where men noticed and valued a woman for her looks and her readiness to submit. In such a social climate, it was only a matter of time before Esther was discovered. She got lost in beauty treatments, perfumed oils, and in her studied, skillful efforts to comply with the wishes of the men in her life.

But life is full of unpredictable twists and turns—long lulls, disappointments, tragedies, and big breaks—that push us out of the shadows and force us to summon up courage, strength, and gifts we never knew we had. Esther's beauty didn't fade or, if it did, no one seemed to notice. Instead, other aspects of her character surfaced, showing the world and proving to Esther herself that she had serious responsibilities before God and a whole lot more to offer than beauty and compliance. When Esther faced the crisis of her life, the powers of face and form were not enough, and her ability to please stood in her way. The situation called for her to think and strategize, to exercise courage, to stand on her own two feet, and to rely solely upon her God. That's when Esther, long lost in her beauty, was finally found.

THE STUFF OF FAIRY TALES

Everyone loves a great adventure story, and Esther's is one of the best. I remember loving to hear her story in Sunday school when I was a little girl. I enjoyed the heroics of Moses, Joshua, and David too. But even back when I was celebrating single-digit birthdays, I always sat a little taller in my chair whenever Esther's story got told.

Unfortunately, Esther's story has all the ingredients of a fairy tale and often gets treated like one — part Cinderella, part Beauty and the Beast. A beautiful maiden comes out of obscurity to win the king's heart and become his bride. The king falls under the spell of an evil villain, but is freed by the courageous resourcefulness of his enchanting queen, as he bends to her wise influence. Perhaps it is our longing for the "happily ever after" in our own stories that leaves us clinging to fairy-tale interpretations of the Bible. But Esther's story wasn't a fairy tale. It was, in reality, much closer to a nightmare.

Even the most lavish and seemingly harmless scenes have a chilling aura of wickedness and oppression. The curtain lifts as the most powerful man in the world, Persia's King Xerxes (whose expansive kingdom stretched over 127 provinces from India to Sudan, 486 – 465 BC), threw a grandiose six-month banquet for his top brass to show off his wealth and possessions. A second lavish seven-day banquet followed in the palace gardens for all the men in Susa. Both banquets were eye-popping spectacles of the glories of his kingdom — extravagant affairs his guests would talk about for the rest of their lives. No one witnessing such staggering exhibits of wealth, power, and luxury was in doubt of Xerxes' might and authority. The world belonged to Xerxes.

A little child once asked the reigning British monarch if her crown was heavy. With the wisdom of a sage, Queen Elizabeth II replied, "It's *supposed* to be heavy." In fact, the British crown was so heavy, generations earlier Queen Victoria ordered a smaller diadem crafted to maintain the proper appearance of a ruler while simultaneously relieving her aching neck. King Xerxes displayed little awareness of the weight of responsibility resting on his brow. Instead of ruling wisely and guarding the welfare of his subjects, Xerxes partied. In making decisions of the gravest import, often involving the fate of human lives, he yielded repeatedly to the silly and sometimes sinister counsel of his closest advisers. He acted sensibly only when he heeded Esther's advice.

Life can be terrifying under the rule of such a man. Scholars tell us that under Xerxes' reign, the Persian Empire was "a society fraught with danger ... ruled by the pride and pomposity of buffoons."[2] The danger this posed to the people of the Persian Empire proved very real and threatening to a beautiful young Jewish orphan girl named Hadassah, who lived under the protective wing of her cousin Mordecai, who adopted her as his daughter. We know this young Jewish exile best by her Persian name, Esther. Hadassah was the first part of Esther that got lost.

The fairy-tale aura of Esther's story vanishes in a puff when the narrator sets her down in a specific place and time in history. Esther lived in Persia, in the city of Susa, located somewhere in southwestern Iran. Her parents or grandparents were exiled when Babylon's King Nebuchadnezzar destroyed Jerusalem in 586 BC. Cyrus the Great of Persia reversed this exile when he allowed the Jews to return to their homeland in 539 BC. Events in Esther's story happened some fifty years after their return. She was among the Jewish people who chose to remain in Persia instead of returning to their native soil.

The book of Esther gives the history behind the Jewish Feast of Purim still observed by Jews today and tells the story of God's unrelenting faithfulness to his people who remained outside the land of Palestine. Within these larger objectives, the book centers more narrowly on one young Jewish girl and God's call upon her life. Her personal history touches the outer fringes of a woman's value and purpose. At her lowest point, she is rounded up like cattle with other young girls without regard to her as a person. At her highest, she sits at the apex of world power and wields a staggering level of influence in international affairs. Her story is truly big enough to contain every woman's story.

THE SEARCH FOR MISS PERSIA

At the height of banqueting, an inebriated king summoned Queen Vashti to parade herself like a beauty pageant contestant before a roomful of drunken dignitaries as a fitting last course—a delicious feast for male eyes—for "she was lovely to look at" (Esther 1:11). As one scholar notes, "Having shown off his wealth and his power, [Xerxes] now seeks to show off his wife, as if she is in the same category."[3] Xerxes' command violated social decorum for any self-respecting Persian woman and hardly suited a queen.[4] Instead of passively doing what she was told, Vashti refused. Following the counsel of his advisers, Xerxes rashly banished her from his presence forever and mandated "that every man should be ruler over his own household" (Esther 1:22)—something the king just publicly failed to do. The Vashti affair set a somber tone for her successor. Xerxes' next queen will think twice before daring to go against the king.

Esther entered the story four years later, when the king's thoughts turned back to Vashti with regret. Sympathetic aides advised him to round up the most beautiful young virgins in the empire to choose a successor for the deposed queen. This segment of the story is appalling. These were young teenage girls. One can easily imagine parents desperately trying to hide their young daughters from the harem scouts. Esther and the other young girls who got caught in Xerxes' net had no say in the matter, but were helpless as slaves. Once brought to the palace, their sole mission in life was to give pleasure to the king—to please his eye, to satisfy him in bed, and to expand his impressive collection of possessions for others to admire.

I wonder that Mordecai didn't throw a burka over Esther and smuggle her out of the country. But perhaps Xerxes' roundup took place without warning. Once Esther was taken, Mordecai's body language reflected his torment over her plight. Like a frantic parent whose young daughter is out well past curfew, he paced outside the harem courtyard day after day, distressed and desperate to hear word of Esther. Meanwhile, she entered a yearlong beauty treatment—marinating in oils and perfumes for twelve months before being served up in her tryst with the king, who rated each girl's performance and decided her fate. The potential for rejection and degradation is difficult to fathom. My Sunday school teacher never explained this part to me.

This marked a turning point for Esther. She chose to play the game. Warned by Mordecai to conceal her Jewish identity, she managed to elude detection and won high marks from everyone inside the palace because she was so pleasing. Hegai, the king's eunuch who supervised the women's care, picked her out from all the other girls as the favorite and took extra measures to promote her candidacy. She complied with everything he said. When her turn came for a one-night stand with Xerxes, she delighted the king more than all the other virgins, won his heart, and walked away with Vashti's crown. Esther was beautiful and pleasing, and she was losing her way. In all her splendor, the beautiful queen was being lulled to sleep.

For the next five years, Queen Esther was the perfect woman—the fairest in the land, dutifully complying with the wishes of her husband and king and never making waves. Remarkably, she even managed faithfully to follow instructions that came from Mordecai, her father figure, who kept an eye on things from the sidelines. This fragile arrangement was bound to collapse and did—in a single day. But instead of destroying Esther's life or getting her in trouble, the crisis shook her awake and proved to be the making of her.

WHATEVER HAPPENED TO HADASSAH?

The first time I began to see Esther's flaws, I felt like I was losing something precious. Here was one of the rare legendary women of the Bible, a real hero of extraordinary valor and bravery whom I truly admired. Then someone had to go spoil it all by pointing out her faults. Over time, I've come to see the value of being as honest about people in the Bible as the Bible is. Their flaws, failures, and sins are on record for a purpose—not for us to gloss over or excuse them or (worst of all) to look down on them because we haven't made the same mistakes. We'll never find ourselves in Esther's story if we convince ourselves she's perfect. Only in seeing her flaws do we find courage to face our own. Through Esther's failings we discover God's heart for flawed people and find hope for ourselves. How disheartening it would be to read a Bible filled with stories of perfect people.

God wants us to see Esther's flaws, and they are big ones. He made Esther beautiful. But this gift, like any other, came with responsibility to use it as a faithful steward in ways that honored him and promoted his kingdom. Inevitably people were drawn to her. She lost her way when she accepted the culture's view that beauty was all she had to offer. She forgot she was Hadassah—a daughter of the covenant, a descendant of Abraham and Sarah, and God's image bearer. She lost her true identity when she made beauty her business. Her purpose slipped from pleasing God to making Xerxes happy, whenever he happened to send for her. According to God's blueprint for women, Esther was seriously off mission.

From another angle, we get a truer assessment of Esther when we compare her to other exiles who faced similar situations. Granted, she was following Mordecai's instructions, and I must confess it is easier to write about Esther's choices from the comfort of my home than to face such dilemmas head on, like she was forced to do. What ghastly fate awaited the one who defied the king? Yet the threat of dire consequences didn't intimidate other exiles who came under similar pressures and, at great personal risk, held their ground out of loyalty to God. They suffered plenty for their choices. Compared with other young Israelites—Joseph in Egypt or Daniel in Babylon—Esther (along with Mordecai) was a compromiser. She didn't display the same passionate loyalty to God or to his people that drove the actions and flooded the prayers of these steadfast youths. Instead, she shed her Jewish name, concealed her true identity, and morphed into the surrounding culture.

Morally, she presents a disturbing picture too. She didn't simply survive her abduction into Xerxes' harem. She made the most of it. She auditioned for the queen's crown by having sex with a man who was not her husband. Then, after winning the tiara, she joined herself in marriage to a pagan man. This happened around the time when, back in her homeland, Ezra the priest was taking drastic measures in Jerusalem to restore the purity of Esther's fellow Israelites. He broke up marriages (families with children) and literally insisted on divorces between Israelite men and foreign women to stave off God's anger for their flagrant disregard of his word.[5]

Meanwhile, back in Persia, Esther kept her secret in the closet. Being a second- or third-generation exile made her cover-up much easier. She learned Persian as a child, so her speech didn't have the telltale Hebrew accent that typically exposed a person's foreign descent. She grew up in Persia, so she, like the Americanized children of U.S. immigrants, was thoroughly local in her dress, conversation, and manners. For five long years, she accepted the sexual mores of the pagan world and enjoyed the luxuries of her privileged lifestyle. "Esther is a passive young woman who tries to live in two worlds. Once she is chosen to be part of the royal harem, she has an identity crisis. This is made clear when she enters the story.... She comes from a religious background, but the whole emphasis in the king's harem is on physical beauty. Esther fits right into the pagan ethos."[6]

Had she followed in the footsteps of her brothers in the faith, she would have switched the timing of her famous "If I perish, I perish" speech to an earlier point in her story. But she was deeply flawed, and the forces behind her choices were complex—a mix of culture, youthfulness, Mordecai's counsel, fierce pressure, and the state of her own heart. God chose her anyway, flaws and all, for his purposes. If he were looking for perfection, he would bypass the likes of Esther or Mordecai, or even Daniel or Joseph, for that matter. He certainly wouldn't be choosing any of us. Esther's story restores our hope that God has important purposes for us all, no matter who we are or how many bad choices we make.

NO EXCUSES

The whole thing came crashing down on Esther's head when a serious conflict erupted between "Mordecai the Jew" and another nobleman, "Haman the Agagite," Xerxes' second in command. Animosity between them quickly spiraled out of control. The two men embodied the age-old struggle between God's people and their enemies.[7] Haman became so obsessed with hatred for his nemesis, even the death of Mordecai couldn't quench his thirst for revenge. He raised the stakes by plotting genocide against Jewish people throughout the Persian Empire. On the first month of the year, Haman cast the *pur* (or lot) to determine when to launch his assault. The lot fell on the twelfth month. True to form, Xerxes carelessly took precious little persuading to give

Haman *carte blanche* to exterminate "a certain people" he portrayed as a threat to the state.

Esther's world turned upside down the day Haman's decree went out. Once again, Mordecai spoke through body language. "He tore his clothes, put on sackcloth and ashes, and went out into the city, wailing loudly and bitterly" (Esther 4:1). Esther dispatched a messenger to find out what was wrong. The messenger returned with the double-barreled news of Haman's heinous plot and a mandate from Mordecai for her to go to the king and "beg for mercy and plead with him for her people" (Esther 4:8).

Suddenly Esther's system of keeping everybody happy no longer worked. She could no longer coast on her beauty or her ability to please. Xerxes and Mordecai, the two most important men in her life, were at loggerheads. She couldn't obey them both. Furthermore, instead of having someone to think for her and to take care of her, Esther must think for and take care of herself. Not only that, hundreds of her people would die if she failed to act. Suddenly a voiceless Esther must find her voice and speak out against atrocities planned against her people, and all within a system that mandated her silence. This young woman who never had to think for herself, take a stand, or fight a battle must stand up to the most powerful man on earth, a man whose strongest political enemies trembled in his presence. And Esther knew all too well what he was capable of doing. She hadn't forgotten what happened to the last woman who crossed him. She had Mordecai's undying support—along with all her people. But the fact remained: Esther must act alone. No one was there to hold her hand or to shelter her.

Initially, she tried to dodge this unwelcome responsibility, reminding Mordecai that the king had not summoned her for a month, and (as Mordecai well knew) the king had one law for any who dared to approach him uninvited: they were put to death. An exception was possible only if the king was in a mood to extend his golden scepter. No one could count on Xerxes to do the right thing, especially if his advisers were whispering in his ear.

Mordecai was noticeably unmoved by Esther's predicament. In light of the looming holocaust, her excuses meant nothing to him. The message he sent back must have sent a chill straight through her:

> Do not think that because you are in the king's house you alone of all the Jews will escape. For if you remain silent at this time, relief and deliverance for the Jews will arise from another place, but you and your father's family will perish. And who knows but that you have come to royal position for such a time as this? (Esther 4:13–14)[8]

Everything the situation demanded went against the grain of her upbringing, her conditioning as a woman, her well-established habits, and her natural inclinations. Mordecai was calling Esther to break the law and risk her life. Her first battle—even tougher than facing Xerxes—was to face and overcome herself.

Once Esther grasped the urgency of her calling, she commanded Mordecai, "Go, gather together all the Jews who are in Susa, and fast for me. Do not eat or drink for three days, night or day. I and my maids will fast as you do. When this is done, I will go to the king, even though it is against the law. And if I perish, I perish" (Esther 4:16). Her first action was loaded with significance, but strangely goes right past us. The transformation taking place in Esther isn't cosmetic, but springs from the core of her being. As one Old Testament scholar observed, "Her response demonstrates that she has not merely been cowed into submission by Mordecai's authority, for it is not one of resigned acceptance but one of firm conviction.... This is a decisive turning point in Esther's development. Heretofore, though queen, she was nevertheless fully under Mordecai's authority as his ward. Now she is the one who sets the conditions and gives the commands."[9] It also marks a major shift in her relationship with Mordecai, who "went away and carried out all of Esther's instructions" (Esther 4:17).

After committing her cause to God's hands, Esther donned her royal robes and braced herself to approach the king. This moment is drained of its tension because we know things turned out well for Esther. *She* didn't know that going in, however. She suffered all the anxieties of a death-row inmate waiting for the governor's last-minute pardon. The prayers and fasting of God's people, joined with trust in God, are no guarantee our lives will be spared. We've lost count of the numbers of faithful, trusting believers who have been martyred for their faith. Hadassah could have easily been one more name on the roster of forgotten martyrs. As she stood in the inner court of the palace and saw Xerxes sitting on his throne, this young woman felt the full force of the terrible possibilities that loomed. Male artists who portray this terrifying encounter often depict a swooning Esther, supported by her maids.

Esther didn't swoon. She did what she had to do. She stepped out. She took the risk. The king (who may have learned something after all from his disastrous mistake with Queen Vashti) extended his scepter and granted her request up to half of his kingdom. This heart-stopping moment turned the tables against the enemies of the Jews and opened a new chapter for Esther. Now, at last, she knew who she was and the cause she was born to advance. There would be no turning back for the queen of Persia.

Old Testament scholars are in awe of Esther's remarkable metamorphosis from a passive, compliant young woman who depends on others to think for her and guide her into a powerful leader of the Jews who displays courage, wisdom, and political savvy. "She begins as a nonentity, valued in that courtly world only for her good looks and her body, but she resolutely accepts Mordecai's challenge to use her position as queen to act for the salvation of her people (with but one brief objection). In one decisive moment she becomes a force to be reckoned with.... Esther, with her courage, cunning, ingenuity, and diplomacy — a woman in a world that was not only ruled by men but devalued women — is the main agent in effecting [the Jews'] deliverance."[10]

ESTHER AND GOD

One of the most troubling aspects about the book of Esther — Hebrew scholars say this is the "genius" of the book — is the fact that God is never mentioned. Neither Esther nor Mordecai speaks his name. There is no thunderbolt from above, no miracle or vision, no heavenly voice. Nevertheless, God is the true hero of the story. Although hidden from view, he is everywhere at work behind the scenes. He keeps his promises and defends his people — even the ones who chose not to return home to the Promised Land. He chooses to work through Esther and Mordecai, despite their failures, bad choices, and outright disobedience. When the crisis hits, he has them right where he wants them. Mordecai is in a corner where he can do nothing except appeal to Esther for help. This was backwards from the way their relationship always operated. Esther is poised for action, yet feels frightened, alone, and inadequate. They were the right people, in the right place, at the right time, and in the right frame of mind. God called them to act. He exposed their need for him, brought them to their knees, and was with them in the battle.

We're amazed to see God providentially lining up people and events to bring about an extraordinary victory for his people. We love to repeat Mordecai's famous life-changing message for Esther: "Who knows but that you have come to royal position for such a time as this?" It's heartening to think that God works like that behind the scenes of our lives too, that he's advancing his purposes through us despite our weaknesses and failings.

Still, I am left with a lot of questions about Esther. What does her life teach me as a woman living in a man's world? What was God showing her about himself and about herself? What was he teaching her about her relationships with men? Does her story have any relevance to me and to the kinds of struggles I face—when I'm making excuses about why I'm the wrong person for the job and backing away from a difficult conversation or situation because I fear what might happen if I step out? Is her story designed to teach me anything about God's call for me to act with courage, or does her message apply only to queens facing international crises? Does she show us how to live for God and, more specifically, how to live for God in a man's world?

Until the crisis, Esther lived by the culture's view of who she was and what gave her value. She had been warned—by Vashti's tragic experience and by Mordecai's solemn warnings—to remain quiet, stay out of trouble, and keep her convictions to herself. She learned from her surroundings and from the people in her life that what truly mattered about her was on the outside. No one looked beneath the surface. No one wondered what gifts God had entrusted to Esther, what vital contributions she was supposed to make. No one engaged her mind, challenged her to think, or counted on her wisdom, insights, and contributions. No one inspired her to look around for opportunities to build God's kingdom. No one needed Esther, at least not for anything significant.

Once in a conversation after church I heard a single woman say wistfully, "I just want someone to take care of me." It sounded strange, coming from an intelligent, talented, well-educated, and wonderfully competent woman. Yet she was simply drawing the only logical conclusion from what she had been hearing in Christian circles—that God created the man to protect, provide for, and lead the woman. An article addressing Christian parents reinforced this thinking when it challenged parents to teach their sons to be bold, courageous adventurers who explore the world and rescue damsels in distress, and to teach their daughters to be gentle, hospitable, and pure.

God wanted more from Esther. He actually put her in a position that compelled her to become a bold, courageous adventurer and do some rescuing of her own. Not only was no one there to take care of her, she had to defend a nation. She protected the king from the wicked counsel of his trusted adviser, Haman. She protected Mordecai and her people by obtaining royal authority to counteract Haman's plot to destroy them. She did a whole lot more than merely imploring Xerxes to prevent the atrocities against her people. The king empowered her, and she acted decisively. She exposed Haman, and her accusation led to his execution. She used her position as queen to advantage Mordecai, for when she revealed their family relationship to Xerxes, the king promptly elevated Mordecai to second in command, the spot Haman had vacated. Subsequently Esther and Mordecai collaborated, issuing orders to end the peril threatening the Jews. Exercising full authority, Esther and Mordecai jointly decreed the feast of Purim to celebrate the Jews' "relief from their enemies, and ... when their sorrow was turned into joy" (Esther 9:22).

Esther wasn't an ornament. She was a leading participant in the major events surrounding God's purposes. The culture wanted her to be beautiful and compliant. God made her beautiful, but he didn't create her for passivity or to satisfy the selfish pleasures of men. Passivity won't take God's image bearer far. Esther had no choice. She had to act. It wasn't simply timing, circumstances, and the urgings of Mordecai that prompted her to act. She was created for this. This was her calling as a woman — to wage war against the enemies of God and fight for his kingdom and his people. God wasn't simply "finding something for Esther to do" — some task so she would feel useful and included. He gave her a *vital* job no one else could do.

The crisis marks an extraordinary turning point in Esther's life and in her relationships with both Mordecai and Xerxes. It is a coming of age when Esther thinks for herself and takes full responsibility for her actions. Her relationship with God flourishes. He is her compass as she navigates the treacherous waters of her relationships with the two most powerful men in her life. By aligning herself with God's cause, she honors both men and leads them both to honor him with their leadership.

AN *EZER* ANYWAY

Esther's relationship to Xerxes was a marriage in name only. Even though she was his wife, she wasn't the only woman in his life. He had a whole smorgasbord of concubines to choose from. No matter how badly she may have wanted to be more to him, it wasn't possible to be part of his life or a strong ally in his battles.

Esther's story is a gift to women who long to be *ezers* in their marriage or in some other significant relationship, but for one reason or another are shut out. Esther was married to a man who didn't share her faith. That in itself isn't always an insurmountable problem. Many women married to unbelieving husbands are a huge blessing and a powerful force for good in their husband's life. But in Esther's case, it was impossible. No matter how much she longed to come alongside and be a force for good to Xerxes, he never let her in. When Esther said, "If I perish, I perish," she was talking about having a conversation with her husband. That's how dysfunctional their relationship was. Her husband didn't want her spiritual partnership. He wasn't interested in her faith or in her advice. If he wanted advice, he consulted his seven foolish advisers. If he wanted encouragement and comfort, he might just send for one of his concubines. Esther might as well have been unmarried, for all the good she could do a husband like Xerxes. Sometimes it's impossible for a woman to be an *ezer* to her husband because he keeps her at arm's length.

But Xerxes couldn't change the fact that Esther was an *ezer*, a strong helper. Even though he shut her out, this was her calling, and she actually became one of the finest examples of an *ezer* we have. Her story gives powerful evidence that the *ezer* isn't limited to marriage. Esther was an *ezer* to Mordecai. She aligned with him in battle, in thinking and in strategizing their next steps together and, yes, even in commanding him from her post in the palace.

THE *EZER* AND THE NOBLEMAN

I fear our marveling over God's providence in putting Esther on the throne "for such a time as this" distracts us from marveling over God's providence in Esther's relationship with Mordecai. His big career break came when he uncovered a plot to murder the king. This was Mordecai's ticket to the top. So it was a painful disappointment for Mordecai when the king promptly forgot his deed of valor and promoted Haman to power. Although Xerxes later realized his oversight and gave Mordecai a day to remember (forcing Haman to parade and honor him throughout the city), God ultimately advanced Mordecai to power through Esther instead.

Furthermore, Mordecai—who sacrificed for, provided for, and protected the young orphaned Esther, and who paced, coached, and sent covert messages after her abduction—reached a point where he had to admit *he* needed her. God used the crisis to bring Esther out from behind Mordecai's shadow and to teach him to depend on her. Mordecai thought all along that Esther needed him. God backed him into a corner where his very life depended on her. God has his ways of drawing men and women into strong alliances.

Which means the corollary is also true, for like Esther, every woman needs a Mordecai. I'm reminded how much I do every time some new challenge confronts me—a job promotion into management, starting my business in England, writing a book, going solo on speaking engagements. By now I should be accustomed to feeling I've gotten in over my head, but it still shakes me up. What a difference it makes when there's a man like Mordecai around—my husband, father, a business colleague, or a close friend—to cheer me on, to be a sounding board and wonder with me if God has put me where I am "for such a time as this." Mordecai summoned Esther into action. He refused to accept her excuses. His voice—more than any other—gave her the courage to move ahead. As women, we are responsible to step out whenever God calls, with or without encouragement from men. How much easier for us when the men in our lives acknowledge their need of our gifts and do whatever they can to empower us to use those gifts.

That Esther commands Mordecai is monumental. His response affirms the rightness of her actions and the godliness of a man who is unthreatened by this "role reversal." He called her to step out, and when she did, he affirmed her by doing whatever she asked.

What she commanded was also significant. Esther committed herself and her maids to a three-day fast before she took any action. She called on Mordecai and the people of God to join this crucial fast—to express sorrow for their sin and cry out to God for help they didn't deserve. She acted as the spiritual leader of her people—leading them back to God to acknowledge their dependence on him. After they do, she will approach the king. So how did this impact Mordecai?

Contrary to fears voiced often today—that a man is diminished if a woman takes the lead—Mordecai only stood to benefit. Esther pointed him to God, saved his life, and fostered his rise to power. That was only the start of the good she brought him. After five years of living and observing palace life, she understood palace politics as an insider. Her skillful handling of the king in the crisis was only the first time her knowledge and experience proved indispensable. Mordecai valued and needed her partnership long after the initial crisis died down.

Together they give us one of the strongest pictures of a Blessed Alliance. Esther was no longer a dependent. Nor was she independent of Mordecai. She was an equal who stood with him in battle. This was God's plan for men and women from the beginning—to rule and subdue together. United, Esther and Mordecai battle to free God's people from the jaws of the Enemy.

STANDING TALL WITH ESTHER

While I was writing this chapter, *Forbes* released its annual list of the "100 Most Powerful Women in the World"—a list Esther would have topped in Persia's glory days. The current impressive list, headed by Condoleezza Rice (then U.S. national security adviser and subsequently secretary of state), includes presidents and heads of state, social activists, politicians, journalists, and first ladies. I can't help sitting a little taller when I see a list like that. As a Christian, I'm even more impressed by the women I know who are following in Esther's footsteps, not by wielding political power, but by fighting for God's kingdom in missions great and small, often at great personal cost and always against the odds—bringing compassion, mercy, justice, and truth into a needy world. An image bearer friend of mine—a dentist by profession—is volunteering for a county dental clinic in the Blue Ridge Mountains of North Carolina, helping indigent people who can't afford to go to the dentist. Author Kay Warren of Saddleback Church and Rosemary Jensen, founder and general director of The Rifiki Foundation, Inc., have been gripped by the needs of HIV/AIDS victims in Africa—especially women whose husbands brought the disease home and children infected and orphaned by their parents. These *ezers* are doing what they can to make a difference for others and, I might add, they all have Mordecais standing behind them and cheering them on.

I still love Esther's story. She makes me feel proud to be a woman—but I have better reasons for admiring her now than I did when I was a child. She is a powerful reminder that God values women and their contributions, and that it brings joy to his heart and blessings to others when his daughters rely on him and embrace the challenges he puts in their path.

Esther is the last Old Testament woman in our study. As we enter the New Testament era, we sense a seismic shift for women. Jesus has come, bringing major changes for women. No longer working behind the scenes, God works out in the open through Jesus. As we observe how Jesus relates to women, we will discover how he changed our lives for the better and how, beginning with his own mother, he will surprise us and lead us deeper into God's great purposes for his daughters.

FOCUS: Like a lot of women today, Esther was lulled to sleep by the culture's anesthetizing message that a woman's value depends on how she looks and on her ability to please others. Esther's story awakens us to the bold biblical message that God values and counts on his daughters as kingdom builders.

ESTHER'S STORY: Esther 1–10

FOR DISCUSSION, READ: Esther 1:1–17, 20; 3:8–10; 4:1–17; 5:1–3; 8:1–8

1. How does the view of women reflected in Esther's story compare with how women are viewed throughout the world today? What are women valued most for today, both in the secular culture and in the church?

2. According to the Persian culture, what did Esther have to offer?

3. How did Esther embrace her culture's view of her? How did it hurt her?

4. Contrast Esther before and after she learned of Haman's edict to exterminate the Jewish people?

5. What made this bold transformation in Esther so unlikely? What changed in Esther to make it possible?

6. How did Esther become a true *ezer*? How did her decisive risk-taking actions affect her relationship with Xerxes and with Mordecai?

7. According to the full story of Esther's life, what was her true value in God's eyes?

8. How does Esther's story show us that God values and works through us to advance his kingdom today? How is she a role model for us?

THE FIRST DISCIPLE—
OF NAZARETH

She was only a young girl, but she was a hero in anyone's book.

No one was less likely to end up in the history books than Blandina, the slave girl martyred in France (AD 177) during a savage uprising against Christians based on sordid, but false, accusations. Eusebius, a fourth-century historian, carefully preserved her legacy as a woman whose devotion to Jesus knew no limits. Others who faced death with her admitted overwhelming fear, including her mistress, who trembled at the prospect that her own "bodily weakness" might cause her to falter instead of boldly confessing Christ. In stark contrast, Blandina, overwhelmed by her love for Christ, was "filled with such power that those who took it in turn to subject her to every kind of torture from morning to night were exhausted by their efforts and confessed themselves beaten—they could think of nothing else to do to her." No one could believe she was still breathing, "for her whole body was mangled and her wounds gaped."[1]

Not only did Blandina endure all that her tormentors devised to break her down, up to the last she offered strength to others by her example and valiant words, including Ponticus, a fifteen-year-old boy who wavered, then at her urgings went bravely to his death. Witnesses reported that "the blessed woman" was magnificent in her ordeal and seemed to gain fresh strength from repeatedly saying to her abusers: "I am a Christian; we do nothing to be ashamed of."[2] She finally met her death when she was dropped into a basket and thrown to a raging bull. The young slave girl, in her late teens or early twenties, left nothing behind. She never possessed any of the things people spend their lives acquiring. She never married or raised a family, realized her girlhood dreams, or lived out her full life expectancy. Yet Blandina possessed everything—and knew she did—because she belonged to Christ. Blandina was not merely a dutiful slave, she was a follower of Jesus and a willing martyr for his cause.

In our endless search for strong, godly role models for women, we usually do not think of checking out the local high school for prospective candidates. Contrary to conventional wisdom, which teaches us to look for role models among Christians who are older than ourselves and to expect less of the young, the Bible often showcases exemplary young people whose hearts belonged to God and who gave up everything to follow him. Despite crushing odds, they held their ground against the Enemy and stood firm, and often alone, in their faith.

We make precious little out of the fact that the woman who plays such a central role in the unfolding of God's plan in history and in the church—Mary of Nazareth—was only a young teenager when first introduced in Scripture. Christmas pulpits tenderly describe the birth of Jesus and may mention Mary's youthfulness in passing, but I'm not sure her young age receives the attention it deserves. To put it starkly, God's redemptive purposes for all humankind dangled by the slender thread of a thirteen- or fourteen-year-old Jewish girl. Who would believe that thread could be so strong?

Mary possessed a tough-minded faith in God and willingly embraced his plan in all of its painful beauty. She was only a teenager, but she also was an *ezer*-warrior. She understood she was a soldier, and that necessarily meant stepping into the line of fire and risking everything. She could not have imagined playing such a vital role and literally changing the course of human history. We're all deeply indebted to Mary, the youthful *ezer* who in one brief conversation answered the call of God and readily chose to risk her life for the advancement of his kingdom.

LOST MARY

It seems almost disrespectful to think of Mary, the mother of Jesus, being lost. But think again. The word *lost* crept into her story early when, freshly promoted from childhood, she heard the angel's words, "Greetings, you who are highly favored! The Lord is with you" (Luke 1:28). With those words, Mary lost her reputation, her dreams, and the respect of the Jewish community. At least initially, she lost the trust of her husband-to-be. And what of her parents? Did they believe her preposterous story of a miraculous nonsexual pregnancy? It is unlikely her family fell for such an outrageous tale. Mary's decision to embrace God's purposes unleashed an avalanche of difficulties and drew her into a disorienting mix of breathtaking privilege and unspeakable pain.

Since fathers often negotiated marriage arrangements when their daughters were still little girls, Mary probably grew up knowing she was going to spend her life with Joseph. Unlike engagements, betrothals were legally binding, and although the couple didn't cohabit until after the marriage celebration, only divorce could break this contractual agreement. Exhilarating as Gabriel's words must have sounded—doubly so for Mary as the woman chosen to bear the promised seed and as a young Jewess who longed for the Messiah's coming — what followed radically altered the course of her life and shoved aside her girlhood hopes and dreams of a normal life with Joseph. Right from the start, the cost was high. So were the risks.

The path marked out for Mary was all uphill with hidden potholes she couldn't anticipate. The picture Mary had in her head at the start of her journey — that *anyone* had for the woman so honored — was nothing like the real story. She never enjoyed the pleasured life of queen mother, basking in the glories of her son and waving her gloved hand to adoring crowds from a gilded carriage. Her pregnancy wounded the people she loved best and jeopardized her reputation and even her safety. Back then, a woman found unfaithful could be stoned to death. In a very real sense, Mary could have become another Blandina. But this was only the beginning. Nine months later, she delivered her royal baby in a smelly stable without even the most basic amenities or the customary female attendants to soothe her brow, grip her hand through the worst contractions, or bathe and swaddle her newborn. After that, it was life on the run, in a desperate effort to save her son from King Herod's vicious plots to destroy a potential rival king.

These disappointments and hazards were mild compared to what lay ahead. It's all well and good to be named the star of the annual Christmas pageant and to appear posthumously on stained glass windows in grand cathedrals all over the world. That hardly compensates and in some ways it trivializes the high price Mary paid to answer God's call when she was so very young.

The angel's appearance and stunning announcement may have caught her by surprise, but despite her youth, Mary was remarkably well prepared for the job. One wonders how she became so steeped in God's Word, so bold in her faith, a girl who never owned or even held a copy of the Scriptures in her hands.

Somehow she didn't let that stand in her way. Unaware of what was coming, she had been preparing for this daunting assignment since she was a little child soaking up the truth about God from what she heard in the temple and from the lips of her parents and other faithful Israelites. This *ezer*-child was arming herself for the battle of a lifetime. Like the young child Samuel, little Mary stored away in her heart the theology of Hannah, which sounded clear as a bell in her Magnificat — Mary's psalm of praise to the God who raises up and brings down, the God who lifted her up with this extraordinary honor (Luke 1:46 – 55).

The theology of a teenager steadied Mary to make the hard choice, to brave the risks and tackle the challenges. The God who spoke through the angel Gabriel was no stranger to Mary, but the well-known God of Abraham and Sarah, Hannah, and King David. Like Hannah, Mary was spiritually equipped for the task of raising such a child. Scholar Timothy George writes, "She nursed him at her breast and nurtured and taught him the ways of the Lord. Doubtless she was the one who taught him to memorize the Psalms and to pray, even as he grew in wisdom and stature and in favor with God and others (Luke 2:52)."[3] She was an *ezer*. She was ready and willing to advance God's kingdom.

Right from the beginning, Jesus brought earthshaking changes to everyone he encountered, but no one more so than the woman who was his mother. The baby Mary carried in her womb, so gloriously heralded by angel voices, turned her private world upside down and brought agonies to her soul worse than she could ever have imagined. Mary got lost in the very place where ultimately she was found — in her relationship with her son.

THE BLESSED MOTHER

If Mary's biography had been published as a separate book, I would have to plead guilty to reading only the first and last chapters. To be honest, most of us tend to have only a seasonal interest in Mary. Every Christmas we pull out and reread the familiar first chapter, the wondrous story of the angel Gabriel's appearance and of Mary's beautiful submission to God's call to be the mother of Jesus. "I am the Lord's [bond slave].... May it be to me as you have said" (Luke 1:38). Of course we prefer the tidied-up version, where the freshly swept stable filled with sweet-smelling hay looks so warm and inviting, and the entire cast of characters glows with joy and contentment, as though this were the perfect way to bring a child into the world. We picture her most often cradling the infant Jesus in her arms — the Madonna and child. Obviously, her whole life was completely wrapped around the simple fact that she was his mother. She was the Blessed Mother, the woman who gave birth to her own Savior.

At Easter, we at least occasionally skim through what we believe was the final chapter of her story where a grief-stricken Mary watched her son tortured and crucified. That chapter gets glossed over too, mainly because we can hardly bear the decibel of her agony. Mel Gibson's portrayal of Mary in *The Passion* gave us a stronger dose of the trauma Jesus' mother endured, but even that fails to capture what she really suffered. For most of us, these two scenes are the sum of what we know about Mary. She's the enraptured mother of the Christ child and the sorrowing mother of the crucified Savior.

My two-chapter view of Mary started to change when I became a mother myself. I don't suppose it's all that unusual for a mother to think of Mary when she's cradling a newborn of her own. That's the point where we sense the strongest connection with her — at least I did. A few years later, I treasured Mary's story in new ways when Allison, then four, was chosen to play Mary in St. Clement's Preschool Christmas pageant in Oxford — one of those priceless moments a mother never forgets. But it was only as I began to enter the complexities of parenting, as I sought to understand my child and work through the evolving, sometimes bumpy phases of a mother-daughter relationship that I became curious about the other chapters of Mary's story. That's when I discovered a side to Mary I never noticed before—the Mary trying to sort out her relationship with Jesus, constantly thrown off balance by things he said and did, who struggled to come to terms with her identity as a mother and as a follower of Jesus. Her son turned out to be more of a challenge than she ever expected.

MARY IN THE MIDDLE

A teenager who seemed drawn to trouble like a moth to the flame once asked his mother if she ever thought about him when he was away at school. After reassuring him that she certainly did, she had to laugh to herself at the notion that she could ever put this child out of her thoughts. The love in her heart and the knot in her stomach made forgetting him impossible.

When a child is hurting or struggling, a loving parent can't help feeling the pain too. Those of us who have watched a little one wheeled off to surgery or had a child break down in sobs because she's gotten left out or wounded by someone's hurtful words know this kind of pain. Mothers of older children continue to experience vicariously the highs and the lows of their teenage and adult children. Our hearts are in our throats as they make those long-awaited launches into adulthood, where the air is turbulent and sometimes there are close calls. The hearts of mothers bleed all over the pages of Ruth Graham's book *Prodigals and Those Who Love Them*. There one mother of a prodigal lamented, "You wake up every morning, not from a nightmare, but to one." Mrs. Graham told of being jolted awake in the middle of the night by anxieties for her son. "I knew there would be no more sleep for me the rest of the night. So I lay there and prayed for the one who was trying hard to run from God. When it is dark and the imagination runs wild, there are fears only a mother can understand."[4]

Jesus never gave his mother a single moment's worry over rebellion, bad choices, or running away from God. But that didn't spare her from worrying or losing sleep over him. In the temple, when he was only eight days old, an elderly Simeon set an ominous tone for things to come when he prophesied to Mary: "A sword will pierce your own soul too" (Luke 2:35). These words usually bring to mind the devastating chapter at the end of Mary's story, when she witnessed the brutal execution of her firstborn. But they also capture the bumpy road that led from the stable to the cross. Those rare accounts of conversations between Jesus and his mother that we find in the Gospels (presumably because Mary later told her story to the gospel writers) are laden with love and riddled with pain. Jesus' remarks always caught his mother off guard and left her pondering his words, trying to figure out what he meant, and to sort through the implications. Exchanges between Jesus and his mother are memorable and chronicle the steps of Mary's journey from a mother to a disciple.

LETTING GO

Anxiety struck suddenly and with force when Mary and Joseph lost track of the twelve-year-old Jesus on their return home from the Passover in Jerusalem. They didn't notice he was missing until they were a day's journey from Jerusalem. It took another whole day to return to Jerusalem and a third to locate him in the temple. They were separated from him for three frightening days. Mary knew firsthand the panic that overcomes a parent when a child disappears in a department store or fails to arrive home from school on time. The mix-up over Jesus happened on the return leg of their pilgrimage to Jerusalem for the feast. Typically, on such a journey, women traveled with the younger children, separate from the men and older boys. Jesus was twelve years old—a pivotal year in the life of a young Jewish boy as he transitioned into manhood, moving from the care of his mother to the tutelage of his father. During this coming-of-age phase, a boy could opt to travel with either parent, and apparently each of his parents thought he had gone with the other. It was an honest mistake.

After days of frantic searching, they found him safe and sound in the temple, calmly listening to the teachers and asking them questions, apparently unconcerned about his parents' distress.[5] His exhausted but relieved mother reproached him for his actions. "Son, why have you treated us like this? Your father and I have been anxiously [sorrowfully] searching for you" (Luke 2:48). When you stop and think about it, Jesus' reply was probably the last thing she expected to hear: "Why were you searching for me? ... Didn't you know I had to be in my Father's house [or about my Father's business]?" (Luke 2:49).

Any parent who has known the relief of finding their child alive and unhurt after "anxiously searching" would be completely floored at such a question, "Why were you searching for me?" What a question! Yet even as a young boy, Jesus had clarity regarding his mission. He was on earth to do his Father's will. He felt his parents should have understood and headed straight for the temple the moment they realized he was missing. "Searching" was unnecessary.

Within the context of the Jewish family, Jesus was right where he belonged—making the appropriate shift from his mother to his father to learn and become active in the family business. Only Jesus wasn't shifting to his father Joseph, but to his Father in heaven. At the early age of twelve (and by his answer) Jesus signaled a turning point in his relationship with Mary and with Joseph. He returned to Nazareth with them. He continued to honor his parents by his obedience. Joseph taught him the carpenter's trade. But the family business Jesus took up belonged to his heavenly Father.

Mary's young son was on a mission, and she couldn't get in his way. Already he understood his primary relationship was not with her or with Joseph, but with God the Father. Jesus' words were clear, but not to Mary. She walked away from the encounter pondering his questions and probably feeling slightly hurt. This wasn't the last time he jarred her with his words and left her wrestling to understand. No doubt Jesus' words jolted Joseph too, the man who stood at Mary's side from the beginning and was himself another reason to call her blessed.

THE BLESSED ALLIANCE

Interwoven into Mary's story is another story waiting to be told. In religious artwork as well as in real life, Joseph and Mrs. Noah are two of a kind. Mrs. Noah was eclipsed by her illustrious husband. Joseph stands in the shadows next to Mary, who, along with her baby, is spotlighted on Christmas cards. He's another unsung hero, the nondescript wooden figure in our family's nativity scene that always gets mixed up with the shepherds. Men like Margaret Thatcher's husband, Dennis, and Queen Elizabeth's Prince Philip could relate to a man like Joseph. They know what it's like to be the sidekick of the *real* star of the story, the forgotten man in the margins. Joseph the carpenter is one of the lost men of the Bible whose story (mostly found in Matthew's gospel) we can't afford to lose.

A lot of men in the Bible don't receive nearly the credit they deserve. Joseph falls into that category. He may have been, as some describe him, "a quiet sort of man," but he looms large in Mary's story. The more I learn about Joseph, the more I am in awe of this incredible man. His response on learning the shattering news of Mary's pregnancy proved just how extraordinary he was. Based on the facts, Mary had betrayed him and broken her vows. Under the circumstances, Joseph had a legitimate excuse for blowing up or becoming vindictive and bitter. He had a legal right to bring her to justice. But Joseph wasn't that kind of man. God had done a work in his heart. He was *righteous*—bent on doing the right thing in God's eyes no matter what it cost him.

Instead of heading straight for the civil court to demand a divorce and give Mary what she deserved, a deeply wounded Joseph took pains to shield her from disgrace. His valor didn't stop there.

When God mercifully revealed the truth about Mary to Joseph, he wholeheartedly joined her in this vital and dangerous cause. Mary was remarkably godly, selfless, and courageous. Joseph was her match. Their story often gets told as though it centered totally on Mary. But here again, when God had a major job to do—and this was the most important one—the team he called together was male and female. Together, Joseph and Mary give us one of the best examples of the Blessed Alliance found anywhere in the Bible. Christians would do well to reflect on the selfless way this man and woman worked together to advance God's cause.

Mary risked her reputation and her dearest relationships. Her whole life went up in smoke and, you could say, she lit the match when she accepted the mission the angel Gabriel presented to her. Yet, Joseph was right there with her no matter how dangerous or difficult her path. He was as firmly committed to God's call on Mary's life as she was. Instead of putting her away, he took her into his home and embraced her as his wife. For months he denied himself the conjugal rights he was legally entitled to enjoy. He even served as midwife at the birth of Jesus and adopted Mary's child as his own.[6] When danger threatened because of Herod's jealous insecurities, Joseph dropped what he was doing, shut down his shop, and relocated to another country to insure their safety. He went against the tide of cultural opinion and denied himself in a hundred ways. He was the ideal sort of husband Paul describes in his letter to the Ephesians, a man who loves his wife as Christ loves the church and gave himself for her (Ephesians 5:25). No one will ever know what it cost him.

Joseph was a man ahead of his time. He came alongside Mary and adapted himself to his wife. According to human convention, this was all backwards. But Joseph was a disciple too. He knew

God had called Mary, and he willingly did whatever it took to help her on her way and to promote her faithfulness. Mary could have been unbearably alone and faced impossible odds to raise her son. Joseph never let that happen. However we define Christian manhood, we must incorporate the likes of godly men like Joseph. What a refreshing message we as Christians could send to a gender-embattled world if men and women in the church partnered together as selflessly as these two did for the sake of Christ.

THE JARRING WORDS OF JESUS

Some of the most significant exchanges between Jesus and his mother slip into the Gospels so unobtrusively they almost escape our notice. But a mother, whose antennae are acutely attuned to her child, picks up signals that pass undetected by others. Jesus had a way of saying things that stuck with Mary. He was never flippant, careless, or rude. To the contrary, in every conversation, Jesus was always thoughtful and intentional with his remarks. Words spoken to his mother served his holy agenda for her. The road she traveled was rocky and steep. His destination—the cross—threatened to completely undo the woman who was the Blessed Mother. Jesus' statements about his mother were designed to deliver her from this inevitable shame and loss and give her an identity that was indestructible. And so he said the unexpected, shocked and caught her off balance. Mary heard and pondered what he said.

Jesus stunned his mother at the wedding feast in Cana when she approached him over a shortage of wine—a social calamity at such an important event. Jesus' reply sounds harsh or disrespectful to us. "Woman, what do I have to do with you? My hour has not yet come" (John 2:4 NASB). In Jesus' day, to address his mother as "woman" was neither rude nor inappropriate as it is today.[7] Later, he tenderly addressed Mary in a similar way from the cross (John 19:26). However, the simple fact that he did not address her as "mother" — which any mom would notice — sent a strong signal to Mary that her relationship to Jesus as "mother" was changing. That doesn't mean his words didn't pierce Mary's heart. To declare: "What do I have to do with you?" or "What do you and I have in common?" must have hurt her deeply. After all, she had given birth to him. He might speak that way to others, but how could he say such a thing to his own mother? Jesus was signaling a further stage of separation from his mother. He was defining boundaries in his relationship with her as he entered his public ministry.[8] He was no longer following his mother's directives, but doing the work of his Father.

Jesus rattled his mother again when she and her younger sons became concerned for his welfare. He was so consumed by his ministry that he wasn't taking proper care of himself — no time to eat or sleep. His health was at risk, and they thought he was "out of his mind." They believed they knew what was best for him, so they went to where he was teaching to restrain him and bring him home. But the crowds were so thick, they couldn't get to him. When word reached Jesus that his mother and brothers were standing outside, wanting to see him, Jesus responded with, "My mother and brothers are those who hear God's word and put it into practice" (Luke 8:19–21; see Mark 3:20–21, 31–35). His words sent a double message their way: first to direct his mother and brothers to focus on what matters most, hearing and obeying God's Word, and second to guide them to a true relationship with him that transcended any biological relationship.

Jesus' words marked a radical turning point for himself and, more significantly, for his mother. He was redefining the family. Biological ties, which predominate all through the Bible, are not the strongest ties for Jesus or for those who follow him. The kingdom of God is not biological, but spiritual. Jesus' family isn't built on bloodlines, biology, or genetics, but on a shared commitment to God and his Word. The family ties that bind

God's family together come from hearing and putting into practice the words of Jesus. Jesus was giving Mary the gospel—the only path to blessedness. Shocking as it sounds, physically giving birth to Jesus ultimately meant nothing if Mary never listened, believed, and lived out the teachings of her son. Her true calling in life—and the only bond with him that endures—was to hear his words and to live by them. Her greatest calling was to follow Jesus and cultivate the family resemblance by becoming like her son. The one who takes to heart the words Jesus spoke regarding his biological mother belongs to the only family in the world that truly matters as a full-fledged brother or sister or mother of Jesus. This is the most important family tree for all of us.

In another context an unnamed woman, deeply moved by Jesus' teachings, desired to honor him publicly by praising his mother. In a sudden outburst, she cried out the words Mary had always expected to hear: "Blessed is the mother who gave you birth and nursed you" (Luke 11:27). Such public tribute to Jesus' mother was surely fitting, for to produce such a wise and godly son was the crowning glory of a mother. This kind of remark would make any mother beam with pleasure. In a culture that measured a woman by the number of sons she bore, and especially in light of Jesus' uncompromising teaching about honoring father and mother, you would expect Jesus to thunder a hearty "Amen!" Instead, Jesus dared to disagree. "Blessed rather are those who hear the word of God and obey it" (Luke 11:28). What did Mary think when she learned what Jesus had said? What was Jesus saying about his mother—the Blessed Mother?

THE BLESSEDNESS JESUS OFFERS WOMEN

I'm a mother too and can't help feeling shaken by the force of Jesus' comments about his mother. I grew up believing my biblical calling as a woman was to become a wife and mother, which was one reason I felt so lost when I was single. Jesus topples some of my convictions by his radical statements. I have to wonder how it would have impacted my struggle if I had ever given much thought back then to his shocking words about his mother. "Blessed rather are those who hear the word of God and obey it." I did not realize it then, but the greatest blessings offered by Jesus to me as a woman—single or married—were fully within reach the whole time.

Jesus zeroed in on two sacred institutions for women—motherhood and family—and redefined them both. According to Jesus, a woman's life is truly blessed *not* when she becomes a mother, but when she hears and obeys his Word. The crowning glory for a woman (as for a man) is to be a disciple of Jesus Christ. This is a woman's true identity and the only path to blessedness. To base our identity on anything else is to stand on shaky ground. But nothing can ever take away from us our calling as disciples of Jesus.

Instead, these treasured roles of wife and mother have become the heart and soul of our lives as women. No matter how successful we may be in other venues, we define ourselves by whether or not we have children. We measure our success as mothers by how well our children turn out. Our families are our pride and joy. We are at a loss (and we lose ourselves) when we don't marry or we can't have children or when our families are less than perfect. Most of the women I know have glaring failures and major disasters in the family they came from or the one they are building. They harbor a secret belief that their lives are ruined, that some aspect of their identity as women has been invalidated, and they have nothing worthwhile to offer others. One woman whose children made horrible messes of their lives confided, "No one will ever ask me for advice about raising children." Ironically, she has a lot of sound parenting advice because God gave her such hard assignments. Jesus calls women to follow him—through the messiness of life that we all experience.

Mary's life wasn't perfect either, despite the impression coming from the halo encircling her head in her portraits. The angel's message brought a sudden end to Mary's hopes for a picture-perfect life when she was barely starting out in life. Sometime midway in her story, Joseph died. The loss of a husband finishes off a lot of women. Toward the end of her story, as Calvary loomed on the horizon, Mary stood on the brink of the worst possible shame for a mother. When her son was crucified as a common criminal, no voice cried out, "Blessed is the mother who gave you birth and nursed you." If Mary's identity and meaning in life depended on motherhood and family, this would destroy her. But Jesus came to save his mother too. And so he jarred her free from her identity as his Blessed Mother and gave her an identity durable enough to outlast the cross.

He did all this without diminishing or taking anything away from motherhood. The Bible pays high tribute to mothers — higher than we even realize. The Redeemer — the hope of the world — came through "the seed of the woman."[9] Major leaders in Israel's history were nurtured from infancy and profoundly shaped as adults by the theology of their mothers. Jesus taught emphatically the importance of honoring one's mother. But he never limited women — his mother or any other woman — to the role of mother. Both Old and New Testaments define women in terms broad enough to encompass every woman's life, from start to finish. We are *ezers*. We are God's image bearers. We are followers of Jesus. We fulfill our highest calling and find our deepest meaning in life when we hear and obey his Word. From Mary's earliest days to the end of her life, she was called to be Jesus' disciple. Nothing could take that away from her.

MARY AT GROUND ZERO

Who was the broken woman leaning on John, the beloved disciple, at the foot of the cross? She had no husband. She was losing her firstborn son, the pride and joy of the family. Had Mary's blessedness come to this? This certainly wasn't the scene she envisioned when the angel spoke that glorious announcement to her more than thirty years before. The disgrace she feared at his birth paled against the shame and disgrace of a mother whose son was executed as a criminal. What Gethsemanes did she suffer in the days before, as hostilities mounted against her son, as he set his face toward Jerusalem, and her heart was stricken with fear? Did the heavens writhe in grief as she wept and begged in vain for the life of her innocent son? Now instead of a jubilant chorus of angels heralding the Savior's birth, a savage rabble demanded injustice: "Crucify him! Crucify him!" As her gaze lifted to see her beloved son dying such a death, Simeon's prophetic sword ripped through her soul.

What is hardest to grasp is how the tortured Jesus, in his agony, could possibly think of anyone but himself. Yet he did. He knew she was there and, out of the depths of his misery, reached out to her again. It is a sacred moment—one final exchange between mother and son. "When Jesus saw his mother there, and the disciple whom he loved standing nearby, he said to his mother, 'Dear woman, here is your son,' and to John, the disciple, 'Here is your mother.' From that time on, this disciple took her into his home" (John 19:26–27).

Who was this broken woman? She was Jesus' first disciple. She had been one from the beginning—as a teenager. She was a hearer and a doer of God's Word. Faced with a hard and costly choice, she blazed a path of faith and courage for all women— young and old—and demonstrated the power of a woman who will risk everything to advance God's cause. Like Blandina, Mary is a hero in anyone's book. She offers teenage girls today a stronger role model than some of the alternatives that beckon them. She sets an example for those of us who are adults too. Mary was the first to believe and lay down her life for the gospel. She was the first to leave all to follow Jesus, first to love him and minister to his body, first to hear and treasure his words, the first to share in his sufferings. Incredible as it sounds, for a brief time Mary had Jesus all to herself. She was his first disciple.

In the epilogue of Mary's story we find her right where she belongs—with John and the other disciples of the resurrected Jesus, waiting for the coming of the Holy Spirit. Like her son, she was focused on her Father's business. Her marriage was over, and her son was gone too. But she still knew who she was. She was the blessed disciple—firmly ensconced as a sister and a mother in the growing family of Jesus. She was at peace. Her life hadn't turned out as she expected, but her identity and mission were intact.

Jesus' word for Mary is the same as it is for women today: "Follow me." It is a way that is open to all of us.

Mary of Nazareth wasn't the only woman whose life was radically transformed by her relationship to Jesus. One of the most interesting women in the New Testament—and one of the most controversial and misunderstood today—is another Mary, this one from Magdala. This Mary wasn't known for her halo. She is remembered for siding with the Enemy.

FOCUS: Mary was the Blessed Mother of Jesus. But her blessedness as Jesus' mother started to unravel when the crowd cried out, "Crucify him!" She helps us discover that our true identity and only sure source of blessedness as women is found in following Jesus.

MARY'S STORY: Luke 1:26–56; 2:1–52; John 2:1–11; Mark 3:31–35; Luke 11:27–28; John 19:25–27; Acts 1:14

FOR DISCUSSION, READ: Luke 1:38; 2:34–35; Mark 3:31–35; Luke 11:27–28; Acts 1:14

1. Who are the Christian women you consider to be role models? Are any of them younger than you? Are any of them teenagers?

2. What are the similarities between Blandina the slave girl and Mary the young mother of Jesus? Why are these young women strong role models for us?

3. What expectations would naturally accompany the honor of giving birth to the Messiah?

4. How did the sword of Simeon's prophecy threaten Mary's blessedness? How would the world view her and how would she view herself after her son's crucifixion?

5. How did Jesus redefine motherhood and family?

6. According to Jesus, what is a woman's true and highest calling? Why?

7. How do Jesus' words to his mother sound to you? (See Mark 3:31–35; Luke 11:27–28.) How does he challenge your own sense of what gives you meaning and identity?

8. How do Jesus' words to his mother encompass the lives of every woman from early childhood to old age? How do we, like Mary, find true blessedness?

APOSTLE TO THE APOSTLES —

Mary

MAGDALENE

She got lost in her past and had given up hope of finding her way back.

She was a serious Christian, active in her church youth group and a regular volunteer for vacation Bible school and mission trips. On the outside, she seemed fine. No one detected the deep secret she harbored inside that was killing her with guilt. She'd heard all the talks and read all the books on Christian purity and had pledged to keep herself pure for marriage.

But the promise didn't hold one weekend at college. A late-night party mixed with too much alcohol—she woke up in the morning with a splitting headache and a guy she hardly knew lying next to her. The deed was done. What she lost in the night she could never get back. Over time she came to understand that Jesus forgave her, but somehow she couldn't forgive herself. She knew others would hold it against her too. In bleak moments, she told herself she'd kissed her own life good-bye. She hadn't yet discovered how much Jesus makes of broken lives.

Mary Magdalene got lost in her past too. In fact, she seemed to have a knack for getting lost. She got lost *twice* in the past — once in her own past and then (oddly enough) in someone else's. Later in her story, it happened again when she lost Jesus. If this were not enough, she seems to be getting lost once more in the present as strange rumors circulate about her.

LOSING MARY

The Bible introduces her as "Mary (called Magdalene) from whom seven demons had come out" (Luke 8:2). There's a whole lot of history packed into that one simple statement. This dark piece of Mary's past distinguishes her from the other Marys in the New Testament and reveals the truth about her background, making her rise to prominence among Jesus' followers all the more remarkable. This truth, however, got lost when somewhere along the line Mary became linked to the "sinful woman" (presumably a repentant prostitute) who anointed Jesus' feet with her tears and perfume, then wiped them with her hair (Luke 7:36–50).[1] Although there is no biblical evidence linking her to Mary Magdalene, this association became so strong English dictionaries define *magdalen* as "a reformed prostitute."

Not surprisingly, the impression of Mary as the "fallen woman" who wept at Jesus' feet has detracted from her true story. She is perceived as a shady biblical character — not a shining star like Mary of Nazareth and other women who had better resumes. Such thinking is a long distance from Jesus' view of things. Despite what others might think of the sinful woman weeping at Jesus' feet or Mary the demoniac or the college coed who kissed her life good-bye, Jesus prizes each of them as his followers and enlists them as kingdom builders. They vividly display the transforming power of his gospel in a shipwrecked human life. Sadly, to this day, a cloud hangs over the Magdalene that still obscures the real Mary from view. Unfortunately, instead of clearing up the confusion about Mary, the clouds surrounding her have only gotten thicker.

Some feminist scholars, troubled by the persistent misportrayal of Mary as a prostitute, have suggested that this was part of an early church conspiracy to suppress women and their contributions. They attempted to set the record straight by putting forward new theories regarding Mary's identity drawn from the New Testament, but also from ancient writings other than the Bible — Gnostic writings[2] such as *The Gospel of Philip* and *The Gospel of Mary Magdala*. They claim these writings portray Mary as the disciple Jesus loved best, the designated leader of the church instead of Peter and, most shocking of all, as the wife of Jesus and the mother of his child. Dan Brown's blockbuster novel *The DaVinci Code* circulated these ideas among a wide popular audience that included (and unsettled) many Christian readers. Brown's storyline alleges, among other things, that the Beloved Apostle in Leonardo Da Vinci's masterpiece *The Last Supper* was none other than Mary Magdalene, Jesus' wife, and not the apostle John as traditionally thought.[3] Mention Mary Magdalene in Christian circles these days, and eyebrows will go up.

Despite her problems with mistaken identity and the current controversy swirling around her, Mary Magdalene is one of the most significant women in the New Testament. Of the women who knew Jesus, only Mary of Nazareth is mentioned more times than the Magdalene. Mary Magdalene enjoyed the enviable privilege of a face-to-face relationship with Jesus, which is the single most important reason to study her. Our arsenal of strong female role models suffers an incalculable loss if we drop her from the list or fail to acknowledge her importance. All four gospel writers identify her as one of Jesus' most devout followers, a bold leader, and a crucial eyewitness of the most dramatic moments in the life of Christ. She appears in nine different lists[4] of women, and in all but one her name heads the list, indicating her prominence among the women. Among the followers of Jesus, Mary's name occurs more often in the Bible than most of the twelve apostles. And these are only starters. So no matter what people are saying about her, it is a big mistake to avoid her. Mary is *a must* for our study.

AN ENEMY OUTPOST

Mary started out on the wrong side of the war. She was an Enemy stronghold, providing food and shelter for the Devil's troops—seven of them in all. According to one scholar, she suffered from "a possession of extraordinary malignity."[5] The Bible offers no particulars about how Mary became demon possessed, how long she lived in that desperate state, or the circumstances surrounding her encounter with Jesus when he delivered her. From what we know of other demoniacs in the Bible, we can safely assume that until she met Jesus, she lived a deranged existence that pushed her to the fringes of society. There may have been erratic episodes when, driven by the dark powers within, she screamed, foamed at the mouth, convulsed, and thrashed on the ground. Normal people tend to avoid someone like that. Perhaps, like the infamous Gerasene demoniac, she lived naked among the tombs or possessed abnormal strength that frightened her neighbors and made futile any attempt to restrain her. Such strength, however, was powerless to break the grip of the seven demons who held her captive. She needed Jesus to set her free.

We also know that *no* demon-possessed person ever went to Jesus for help. The sick desperately wanted his help. They traveled for miles, disrupted his work, pulled up roofs, badgered him, and generally made nuisances of themselves just to get to him. But no demoniac ever sought him out. Usually someone else—a desperate parent or a compassionate friend—went to Jesus on their behalf. Sometimes, without being asked, Jesus simply intervened. Around Jesus, the demon possessed were defiant and resistant. Mostly they wanted him to go away.

Mary wasn't seeking Jesus. Her story isn't about the lost lamb who found the Shepherd, but of the Shepherd who searched and rescued this lost lamb despite her determination to avoid him. It is possible she had no family or friends—no one on their knees pleading for God to deliver her. Jesus' strong arm reached into the black darkness that engulfed her and pulled her out to safety anyway.

What a powerful encouragement for those of us with loved ones who have no time for God, who resist the gospel and simply want to be left alone. Most people hold out little hope for someone like Mary, but Jesus doesn't give up on hopeless cases, and neither should we. There's no telling what he will do. Mary's lostness ended the day she met Jesus. He brought an abrupt end to her savage bondage, restored her to her right mind, and freed her to follow him. Never in her wildest dreams could she have imagined where that road would lead.

A FOLLOWER OF JESUS

It's amazing how many times we can read a passage of the Bible before the words actually sink in. That happened to a friend of mine who told me she read her Bible through many times before noticing that Anna was a prophetess (Luke 2:36). I have to admit that it was a long time before it dawned on me that there were actually women who traveled with Jesus and the Twelve. I always envisioned a party of thirteen. But there it was in the Bible for all to see:

> Jesus traveled about from one town and village to another, pro-
> claiming the good news of the kingdom of God. The Twelve
> were with him, and also *some women* who had been cured of
> evil spirits and diseases: Mary (called Magdalene) from whom
> seven demons had come out; Joanna the wife of Cuza, the man-
> ager of Herod's household; Susanna; and many others. These

women were helping to support them out of their own means. (Luke 8:1–3, emphasis added)

Mary is best known for her leading role in the events surrounding Jesus' death, burial, and resurrection. Luke's reference to her here is another often overlooked piece of information that is necessary to make sense of her story. After Jesus delivered her, instead of sending her on her way, he brought her into the fellowship of his followers. She became part of a privileged group of women from Galilee[6] who, along with the twelve disciples, accompanied Jesus as he traveled and ministered from town to town. Ensconced within this inner circle of disciples, Mary had a front-row seat for Jesus' ministry and teaching.

From here, the once ostracized and isolated Mary discovered the meaning of belonging and relationship. Mary's real story is found by looking more closely at her relationships with Jesus and with the twelve apostles. Her relationship with Jesus resulted in the transformation of a useless, self-destructing life into a masterpiece of his grace. She became a key contributor to the advancement of his kingdom and someone to whom all Christians are indebted. Mary and the other women from Galilee were not incidental to the stories of Jesus' male disciples either. These women had a profound, life-changing impact on the Twelve.

"RABBONI!"

Mary wasn't the sinful woman who anointed Jesus, but she had just as much reason to weep tears of gratitude at his feet. Instead of weeping, Mary and the other women from Galilee turned their gratitude into action. They found a vital way to minister to Jesus and his apostles by supporting them out of their personal resources. Who knows how many more lives were touched, how many more people were exposed to the teachings of Jesus, how often a weary Jesus and his fatigued disciples were refreshed and revived because of the kindness of these women? In the process of caring for Jesus, they soaked up his teaching and were on the scene to witness his character, ministry, and miracles.

Our twenty-first-century perspective makes it harder to detect the drastic changes Jesus was introducing to women's lives. Within the first-century patriarchal culture, women led more sheltered lives and moved in a separate, more confined sphere than men. In Mary's world, men and women didn't freely associate together as we do today. Men tended to avoid public encounters with women, which explains why Jesus' disciples were dumbfounded when they found him talking with the Samaritan woman (John 4). Also, education was a male privilege. A woman could pick up a lot from synagogue teachings and from her father, if he chose to teach her. But women never studied under rabbis and, church historians tell us, "it would have been unheard of for women to travel with a rabbi."[7] Also, women didn't have a voice in legal matters and were not accepted as credible witnesses in a court of law.

In these matters, and many others, Rabbi Jesus radically broke with tradition. He didn't isolate himself from women like other rabbis. He taught them openly, engaged their minds, recruited them as his disciples, and counted on them in weighty matters. He gave his male disciples a lot to think about when they heard him teaching women the same deep theology he taught them. Furthermore, instead of dismissing women as legal witnesses, Jesus affirmed them as key witnesses to the most crucial events of human history—his own death, burial, and resurrection.

When Mary recognized the resurrected Jesus, she cried out, "Rabboni!" or "my teacher" (John 20:16). When we put that piece of information together with the snippet from Luke's gospel telling us that Mary was one of the women who traveled with Jesus, it is clear that Mary was a student in the school of Rabbi Jesus. She was blessed with more than the average opportunities to hear his word and to observe and interact with him.

WHY BRING HER ALONG?

I can't help wondering what the Twelve thought of this arrangement. If their response to Jesus' conversation with the Samaritan
woman is any clue, it had to be unsettling to have women in
their party. I must admit I'm a little stunned by it myself, perhaps
because I'm in the habit of thinking Jesus focused exclusively
on the twelve men. Why did Jesus include Mary and the other
women? Was he just trying to be fair? Was this some early form
of affirmative action? Why couldn't the women just listen whenever a crowd gathered or when Jesus taught them occasionally in
private, as he did with Mary of Bethany? Even that was a radical
departure from tradition. Why did he have to bring them along?

When we come across information like this in the Bible, it's
easy for us to think we've uncovered more ammunition for the
ongoing gender war. Maybe the women were being trained for
the same leadership posts as the men. On the other hand, maybe
they were only bringing hot meals to Jesus and his male disciples
and making sure there were enough blankets to go around at
night. This never-ending debate takes our eyes off Jesus and distracts us from noticing the deeper ways his actions were impact-
ing the lives of the men and women who followed him.

Jesus was on a strategic mission. He had come to reveal his
Father to his followers and to draw them into a real relationship
with himself. He was creating a family and he had precious little
time to work. For a brief three-year period, his followers enjoyed
a face-to-face relationship with the Son of God. Their relationship with him involved far more than knowing more about him
than everybody else. The call to follow Jesus carried the ultimate
purpose of becoming *like* him. Discipleship entailed enormous
responsibility. The rest of Christendom (including us) depended
on Rabbi Jesus' students. Their job was to pass on to us what
they learned from him, by teaching us what he taught them and
by loving one another as he loved them.

Their time with Jesus was intense. He filled their minds with more than they could possibly absorb. The apostle John wrote later that if they had written down everything Jesus did and said, "even the whole world would not have room for the books that would be written" (John 21:25). Jesus placed his disciples in situations where they were compelled to live out what they were learning — crises where they feared for their lives, perplexing situations where they didn't know what to do next, and especially in relationships where he dismantled their prejudices and tore down long-established social, cultural, and ethnic barriers. Jesus' ways were *not* the ways of the world. He was blazing a different path for those who follow him.

Occasional encounters with Jesus were not enough to prepare these men and women to carry his mission forward after he was gone. They needed prolonged, sustained exposure to Jesus. In short, they needed to live with him. There was far too much for one mind — or twelve — to absorb. His followers needed multiple perspectives — men and women from different walks of life and social classes. Jesus was forging them into a family, a body, a community, a church whose trademark was to be their love for one another. Mary was in the thick of it all, and Jesus had a vital role for her.

THE PEOPLE JESUS CALLED TO LOVE ONE ANOTHER

Jesus couldn't have chosen a group less likely to coalesce. His followers were a preview of the church — male and female, rich and poor, professional and working class, the right and the left — a motley crew who, without changed hearts, could never come together. Even among the Twelve there was enormous potential for friction and conflict. Jesus called Peter, Andrew, James, and John away from their fishing boats to follow him. Then he put them with Matthew, where natural hostilities existed. Matthew boarded up his tax collector's toll booth and left a lucrative (albeit dishonest) career to become a disciple. He had been overtaxing his own people, including the fishing industry, for the Romans and pocketing the excess to enrich himself. Simon the Zealot would have zero tolerance for a man like him, but Jesus called Simon too.

Jesus called twelve men to follow him. There is no getting around the fact that these men were a central part of Jesus' strategy. They shouldered enormous responsibility when he was gone. But Jesus wasn't starting up a male fraternity or a monastery for men. The church isn't male only, and Jesus isn't building his kingdom with only male help. What God said in the beginning held true for his disciples and is still true today in the church: "It is not good for the man to be alone." The *ezer* is vital here too. And so Jesus chose women to follow him as well. Women like Mary—the lunatic Jesus rescued from the prison of demon possession. The Twelve no doubt saw the "before" and "after" Mary, never expecting her to become part of their company. But her involvement fit the blueprint God established in creation when he called his image bearers—male and female—to serve him and reflect his image *together* (Genesis 1:26–27). Before the story was over, these twelve men would discover their profound need for the women who followed Jesus.

LOST AGAIN

During events surrounding Jesus' crucifixion, Mary Magdalene got lost again. If she had been in trouble earlier, this was the apocalypse. She had undoubtedly witnessed tense moments between Jesus and the religious leaders before, when she must have literally held her breath. This time things were different. He was silent. He did not resist. She, like all the others, stumbled over his words about the cross. What he said about rising from the dead hadn't registered either. Once things started to unravel, there was no stopping it. It was all a terrible nightmare. Watching Jesus die was like watching the end of the world.

All four gospel writers reported Mary Magdalene's presence near the cross. Unlike the disciples who fled and denied him, Mary and the women from Galilee stayed with Jesus to the bitter end (John 19:25; Luke 23:55). This was not a safe place to be, and we should never minimize the fortitude it took to stay there. Nor should we explain away their actions by talking about simple good-hearted devotion. Danger was everywhere in this rough and violent setting, especially for those who identified themselves with Jesus. The male disciples' reactions to the crisis show how terrible and dangerous things were. The heat of battle between the seed of the serpent and the seed of the woman blazed white hot at the cross. Throughout Jesus' sufferings, death, and burial, a squadron of *ezers* remained close by, fulfilling their God-given creation mandate as daughters of Eve. Even for Jesus, in his humanity, it was not good to be alone.

In fairness, the men were probably in greater peril than the women because the authorities would perceive them as a more serious threat. I even wonder if what threw them into a panic was Jesus' refusal to fight back. They seemed ready enough to take up arms,[8] but hardly knew what to do when Jesus gave himself up. To their credit, none of them made these or any other excuses for their conduct afterward. Nor did they take anything away from the raw courage of the women who refused to abandon the dying Jesus. Without dodging their own failure, gospel writers highlighted the faithfulness of the women and did not shy away from the shameful contrast this made with their own conduct. Jesus used their failure to humble his brothers and prepare them to be gentle under-shepherds of his flock and better brothers to these women. There is no more talk about who of them will be the greatest in his kingdom. Now their hearts are better prepared for the major changes his gospel will bring to them personally and are ready to acknowledge their need for others.

The Scriptures don't disclose Mary's thoughts or reactions as she stood by helplessly and watched her Lord suffer and die. But the vicious brutality she witnessed was the kind of life-altering trauma that scars a person for life. No matter what happened afterward, Mary never erased those horrifying images from her memory. Remarkably, she remained throughout the entire ordeal, until it was over, the lights were turned out, and everyone else had gone home. In a moving description, filled with gentleness and grief, Matthew wrote that "Joseph [of Arimathea] took [Jesus'] body, wrapped it in a clean linen cloth, and placed it in his own new tomb that he had cut out of the rock. He rolled a big stone in front of the entrance to the tomb and went away" (Matthew 27:59–60). With sagging shoulders and a heart of lead, Joseph retreated into the night. The sound of his footsteps grew fainter in the distance, along with the glow from his lantern, until all was still and dark. Then these words: "Both Mary Magdalene and the other Mary were sitting nearby watching" (Matthew 27:61 NLT).[9]

TAKING CARE OF JESUS

If Jesus died in our day, we would hold a memorial service, leave flowers and tender notes by his grave, organize a candlelight vigil—anything to express our feelings and get a little closure. Mary and the other women from Galilee had a similar impulse. Here was one last chance to minister to Jesus, though with heightened security around his tomb even this was risky. They planned to return to his tomb as early as possible after the Sabbath to anoint and embalm his body. After his burial, the women went home and prepared spices and perfumes. Then there was nothing to do but ache and wait.

John's gospel breaks the silence regarding Mary in the events that followed, zooming in to give us a close-up of the grief-stricken Magdalene. Sunday morning, while it was still dark, she roused herself (had she slept at all?), rummaged around to get herself ready, gathered up the spices and perfumes she had prepared, and set out with the other women for the tomb. This was to be another grateful anointing of Jesus with perfume and tears.

It's hard to imagine the extreme mood swing the women were about to experience. They expected to see the tomb just as Joseph had left it. So it was a terrific shock to see the heavy stone slab removed—lifted out of the groove and lying flat on the ground—and Jesus' body missing. Immediately they assumed foul play. Evidently Mary took one look at the empty tomb and ran to alert Peter and John. Agitated and breathless from running, she told the two disciples, "They have taken the Lord out of the tomb, and we don't know where they have put him!" (John 20:2). By the time Mary made it back to the tomb, Peter and John had already come and gone. Alone now, feeling lost and beside herself with grief, Mary's sorrow surged and she sobbed without restraint. Jesus was dead, and someone had taken his body away.

"WOMAN, WHY ARE YOU CRYING?"

My daughter's first Bible storybook contains a joyous watercolor of Mary at the moment when the resurrected Jesus speaks her name. The exuberant look of surprise on Mary's face is priceless and makes me smile every time I see it. It's one of my all-time favorite moments in the Bible—the worst of sorrows changed in an instant to the best of joys. We want all of our sorrows to end like that. We're sobbing our hearts out. We can't find Jesus. We've lost all hope. Then Jesus comes. He speaks our name. Suddenly the cloud lifts and our troubles are over. We feel a rush of exuberance. Jesus seems so near, and life is on the upswing again. It fits so well with the "happily ever after" we keep chasing.

Jesus' resurrection is the big moment in the Bible—the central event of Christianity. According to the apostle Paul, everything we believe hangs on this one event. Without it we have nothing—only foolish dreams.[10] After the celestial extravaganza at Jesus' birth, when the multitude of angels chorused the glorious news and overwhelmed the shepherds, I'd expect something significantly more spectacular at his resurrection, certainly something on a far grander scale than a private meeting with one woman.

Why would Jesus start by appearing first to a bereft Mary Magdalene? Why would he entrust this vital, history-altering revelation to a woman who, according to society's rules, wasn't even a credible witness? Just think, if he had only arrived a little earlier, he could have revealed himself to two of the greatest apostles, Peter and John. Wouldn't that have been better? Yet Jesus chose Mary, and from what we know of Jesus, neither his timing nor his choice was an accident. Mary was a perfect choice for the supreme honor of being first to see the risen Christ—fitting, strangely enough, because of her past and also because she was a woman.

MAKING GOOD ON AN OLD PROMISE

After being held for who knows how long in the power of seven of the Enemy's minions, who better than Mary to be the first to witness Jesus' decisive victory over Satan? She knew from painful personal experience just how formidable the Enemy really was. Jesus did far more for Mary than simply free her from demons. By his death and resurrection, Jesus not only broke the power of sin and death, he vanquished her former tormentor, the Devil.

The outcome of the war between the seed of the serpent and the seed of the woman was decided here. And how fitting for Jesus to ask Mary, "Woman, why are you crying?" Although it seems an odd thing to ask in a cemetery, in this case, the question was profound. Mary was weeping over the empty tomb, the one event in all of history that brings hope to all our tears. If

Mary had found what she was looking for—a dead Jesus—we would all have reason to weep in despair. Instead, he was the victor. Hope is alive, no matter how grim things look, and, as my husband often reminds me, Jesus won the war, and the rest of history is simply mopping up. Satan is a defeated foe, and Mary's liberation was complete.

Furthermore, as a member of the fairer sex, Mary belonged to a long line of women that began back in Eden, women with a vested interest in the promised seed. Eve received the promise that the seed of the woman would crush the serpent's head. By faith, the elderly Sarah gained strength to conceive Isaac, the son of promise. Tamar, the righteous Canaanite, valiantly risked everything to preserve the promised line that was dying off under Judah's watch. Hannah, through her son Samuel, nurtured the royal line of David with her profound theology. And the teenager from Nazareth offered herself as the bond slave of the Lord to become the mother of Jesus. And this is only the short list of the women who fought to preserve and protect the promised seed. Now, at last, that very old promise was fulfilled in Jesus. How fitting, then, for a woman to be the first to celebrate the victory of the seed of the woman.[11]

But Jesus had another honor in store for Mary. Not only did he choose to see her first, he authorized and commissioned her to proclaim the good news of his resurrection to his brothers, the eleven apostles, no less. In recognition of her encounter with the risen Jesus and the assignment he gave her, distinguished men down through the ages have bestowed upon Mary the title "apostle to the apostles."[12] A Scottish pastor in the puritan tradition, A. Moody Stuart (1809–98), writes, "She was privileged to follow Jesus to Jerusalem, to look on his cross, to watch at his tomb, to be the first witness of his resurrection, and even to be sent by him as the messenger of his word, an apostle to the apostles themselves."[13]

"GO AND TELL MY BROTHERS"

For Jesus' male disciples, the road from the Last Supper to the resurrection morning was littered with miserable failures. One of them betrayed him. Three nodded asleep repeatedly in Gethsemane even though the agonizing Jesus urged them to watch and pray. When Jesus was arrested, another drew his sword along with a rebuke for failing to grasp the nature of Jesus' kingdom. Then they fled into the night. The last anyone saw of Peter that night was in the courtyard of the high priest where, despite his adamant pledge of loyalty to his Lord, three times he denied he even knew Jesus. Only John was present at the crucifixion. No one knows the whereabouts of the others.

Anyone who has ever felt oppressed by guilt will have some sense of the "if onlys" tormenting the Eleven after Jesus' death. Peter, we know for sure, wept bitterly over his share of wrongs. No doubt the others were under a terrible cloud of guilt too. Jesus appointed Mary as the bearer of good news to this hurting group of men. "Go ... to my brothers and tell them, 'I am returning to my Father and your Father, to my God and your God'" (John 20:17).

It was an awkward assignment, to say the least, for the woman who stoutheartedly stayed through the entire ordeal to address the men who succumbed to their fears and retreated into hiding. That fact alone should have made her comforting words more believable, since the Eleven might have expected an icier message from her. Yet in the healing message she delivered, Jesus affectionately called them "brothers." Her message brought relief and forgiveness to them and diffused any cause for resentment toward the men that the other women might have had. Strangely, her mission didn't go well. After so many deeply regretted failures, the Eleven added one more—that "they did not believe the women"—not Mary or the other women who announced the resurrection—"because their words seemed to them like nonsense" (Luke 24:11).

A VITAL COLLABORATION

Culturally, it would have been acceptable for the apostles to marginalize the female followers of Jesus after he returned to the Father. It wasn't acceptable to Jesus. Throughout Mary's story, Jesus was making value-laden statements about women that went against the culture's view of them. He clearly expected the men who followed him to see things his way and to value the women as he did. Women weren't ancillary, but crucial to Jesus. He didn't give them small jobs. He gave Mary two of the most significant — as the first witness to his resurrection and as an apostle to the apostles.

One of the first matters of business when Jesus appeared to his male disciples was to establish the testimony of the women (Luke 24:22–27). He had already elevated women by including them as his disciples. Now he affirmed their ministries too. They were his messengers. He gave them his word, and their message carried his authority. A lot was at stake if the men refused to rely upon the women's word. At a personal level, the men forfeited the reassurance of Jesus' love and forgiveness when they refused to believe Mary's message. Had they persisted in rejecting the women's testimony, the whole church would have paid a terrible price, for significant portions of the Bible would be missing if the disciples hadn't fully embraced the validity of women as witnesses.

Jesus entrusted the women with vital information about himself that the men needed to know. His apostles could not understand, much less preach or write about, the core events of Christianity — Jesus' birth, death, burial, and resurrection — without learning from the women. Without minimizing the work of the Holy Spirit in inspiring the authors of the New Testament, it is still fair to say that the men who penned the Gospels couldn't write the first and final segments without collaborating with the women who were there and had eyewitness information. Luke openly described the amount of research he did to assemble his gospel (Luke 1:3) — research that doubtless included careful interviews with Jesus' mother, Mary Magdalene, and the other women.

Both Luke and Matthew, the only gospel writers who tell us about Jesus' birth, were completely dependent on Mary of Nazareth to reconstruct the narratives about that phase of his life. She could tell them all about the angelic announcements, the complications and events surrounding the births of John the Baptist and Jesus, and of Jesus' early life. Long discussions with Mary preserved her cousin Elizabeth's story as well as Joseph's and her own.

All four gospel writers relied heavily on Mary Magdalene and the women who were with her for vital particulars concerning Jesus' death, burial, and resurrection. Even John, who witnessed Jesus' death, included many details in his gospel that he learned from Mary Magdalene as she told him her story. Based on John's admission of having to be selective in choosing what to write and what to leave out (John 21:25), it is entirely plausible that some of the parables and miracles that have special relevance for women made it into the final copy because Mary and the other women recalled them.

Jesus' brothers needed their sisters in other ways as well. They faced certain suffering and persecution. Despite their earlier failures, many of them went on to give their lives for the sake of Christ. They needed from their sisters in Christ the same kind of spiritual and moral support the women offered Jesus when they stood with him in his final hours. Peter seems to have understood this, for when the angel released him from prison he headed straight for the home of Mary, John Mark's mother, where he found a group of believers praying for his release (Acts 12:1–17). Jesus' tender words from the cross to his mother and to John are usually interpreted as intended for Mary's benefit. "Dear woman, here is your son," and to John, "Here is your mother" (John 19:26–27). Men who have benefited from the spiritual wisdom and godly counsel of their mothers and other women will concur with me when I suggest Jesus may have done this as much for John's benefit as for Mary's.

Then there was the vast mission Jesus spread before his disciples prior to his ascension—a further refinement of the Cultural Mandate God gave Adam and Eve to rule and subdue and to be fruitful and multiply. Jesus' Great Commission was equally grand in scope. "Go and make disciples of all nations, baptizing them in the name of the Father and of the Son and of the Holy Spirit, and teaching them to obey everything I have commanded you" (Matthew 28:19–20).

A job this size demands the full efforts of every follower of Christ—both male and female, young and old. How could they imagine tackling such a monumental task with only half of the body of Christ engaged? Jesus' first act after his resurrection was to mobilize the women and send them to their brothers. The Blessed Alliance was intact and vital to the success of the spread of the gospel. God's method of operation hasn't changed from creation to the present. He calls men and women to join forces in serving him together.

Mary Magdalene may have been lost in her past, but Jesus gave her a future. Her love for him and zeal for his kingdom intensified because he had done so much for her. The same could be said for the sinful woman who wept at his feet and the college coed who wept in secret. Jesus gave them a future too—an honored place in ministering to his body and in building his kingdom in the world. Instead of limiting Mary's options for ministry because of her questionable past, Jesus expanded her opportunities to serve him and gave her powerful opportunities to minister to her brothers. Her story sends a message to us—not merely that our gifts and ministries are important to Jesus and to his church but that they are *essential*. His disciples learned the hard way how important the contributions of the women were to them personally and to their ministries. What a terrible loss it would have been for the kingdom if the women had retreated to the safety and comfort of their homes instead of following Jesus and entering the battle alongside their brothers.

The apostle Paul and Mary Magdalene had a lot in common. Both started out by siding with the Enemy. Mary was a demoniac. Paul was bent on destroying the church and made a career out of persecuting believers. Neither was a seeker. Mary wanted Jesus to go away. Paul wanted to destroy him and was on a terrorist mission to Damascus when Jesus brought him to his knees. Jesus radically transformed them both from the inside out. Paul, a single man whose critics today regard him as a chauvinist at heart, experienced a radical overhaul with surprising results, particularly on his views of women.

So how did Paul's views of women change? Did he ever buy into the notion of the Blessed Alliance? The answer may surprise you.

FOCUS: Those who knew Mary, the deranged demoniac, would never have imagined her becoming one of Jesus' strongest followers. Her life demonstrates how much Jesus makes of broken lives. Mary Magdalene shows us the vital responsibilities Jesus places on women's shoulders and how crucial we are to his church.

MARY'S STORY: Luke 8:1–3; Matthew 27:55–61; 28:1–10; Mark 15:40–47; 16:1–11; Luke 24:1–12; John 19:25; 20:1–18

FOR DISCUSSION, READ: Luke 8:1–3; Matthew 27:55–61; Luke 24:9–11; John 20:1–18

1. Why do you think the past has such a strong hold on us, even though we are certain of our forgiveness in Christ? Why is it so hard to forgive ourselves?

2. What made it so unlikely that Mary Magdalene would become such a significant leader among the followers of Jesus?

3. What do Jesus' interactions with Mary tell us about Jesus' view of women?

4. Why is it significant that Jesus had *both* men and women among his followers? Why did they need each other?

5. What do we learn about Mary as she steadfastly remained with Jesus throughout his death and burial?

6. Can you relate to her unwillingness to leave until everything was finished? Why?

7. Jesus clearly chose Mary to be the first to see him after his resurrection. Why was his choice of Mary so important and significant?

8. How does Mary's story teach us that we are messengers to others of the gospel of Jesus Christ—the good news that Jesus has defeated the Enemy without and the enemy within—that we follow a living Savior?

RECOVERING THE BLESSED ALLIANCE— PAUL AND THE *Women* OF PHILIPPI

When a partnership collapses, everybody loses.

While vacationing in Victoria, British Columbia, my parents along with my brother and his family hired a carriage drawn by a team of beautiful horses for a tour around the city. It was an ideal way to take in all the sights and experience the quaint British flavor of this Canadian "City of Gardens"—ideal, that is, until the carriage veered too close to the side of the road. One wheel went up on the curb and with a sudden jolt bounced back onto the road, jarring all the passengers and spooking one of the horses into a desperate panic. In a flash, both horses were out of control, racing wildly through the streets of Victoria with terrified passengers fearing for their lives. To make matters worse, the inexperienced driver was helpless to regain control of the frantic animals.

Pedestrians watched in horror as the wagon flew recklessly down the street, like a runaway scene from an old TV Western. At a curve in the road, one horse stumbled, fell, and was dragged for yards by the other horse before the carriage finally skidded to a stop. When the dust settled, the shaken passengers were unhurt, but the injured horse lay on its side in the road, heaving helplessly. Nearby, the agitated second horse stood panting, nervously pawing the pavement.

When the Bible tells us "two are better than one," most of us think of a man and a woman working together. In a perfect world, surely the combination of males and females working in tandem would always be a beautiful sight. But in our fallen, broken world, relationships between men and women (not just in marriage, but in other settings as well) are often characterized by tension, distrust, and hurt, even in Christian circles. Instead of the Blessed Alliance God intended from the beginning, relationships between men and women are strained and can be as awkward and unwieldy as a team of runaway horses, with equally disastrous results.

Although the Fall divided us from God and disrupted the Blessed Alliance, God never gave up on us. He sacrificed his beloved Son to bring us back to himself and to restore the unity he intended for us to enjoy with one another. As his image bearers, our calling is to reflect the same extraordinary oneness experienced throughout all eternity within the Godhead—as Father, Son, and Holy Spirit delight in each other and work together in perfect harmony.

Throughout Scripture we catch glimpses among God's people of how powerful and magnificent the Blessed Alliance can be as men and women band together to advance God's kingdom. We saw this Blessed Alliance surface in a mother and son, as Hannah and Samuel invested themselves to build God's kingdom in Israel. It reappeared when cousins, Esther and Mordecai, stood together against the enemies of God's people. Mary and Joseph, a husband and wife team, displayed that uncommon alliance when they set aside their personal interests, hopes, and dreams to sacrifice for Jesus.

Jesus is still in the business of bringing men and women together. He called his followers to rely on one another to fulfill his Great Commission by making disciples of all peoples. Yet still today we have a hard time maintaining this unity. Sadly, Christian relationships reflect the same breakdown between men and women that we find within the wider culture. Divorce rates among Christian couples keep pace with rates in the secular community. Troubled, disappointing relationships that never appear in divorce court have reached epidemic levels within Christian circles. In the church, relationships between men and women are often tense and hurtful too.

As I travel around the country speaking in churches of different denominations, I've been deeply touched but not entirely surprised at the number of women who express frustration and pain. They often feel lost in the church and can't understand why there's so little interest in the gifts God has entrusted to them. They feel quarantined into children's or women's ministries instead of being included in the wider ministries of the congregation. I rarely come away from a church conference without someone voicing these concerns. At one conference a woman pulled me aside and said in a hushed voice, "Something is very wrong here." These women are not agitating for control of the church. They are concerned about their stewardship to Christ, mindful of the magnitude of our mission and of how serious a matter it is to Jesus when one of his followers buries his or her talents in the ground.

Instead of offering the world a stunning picture of how men and women value each other and serve God together—sharing the load, drawing on the strengths and gifts of every member of the body, and ministering together in unity—we divide and minister along gender lines. We view men's gifts as vital to the church. In contrast, we caution women to exercise their gifts discreetly to avoid causing problems or trespassing some invisible line—which changes location from church to church, sometimes even within the same denomination. Like the woman said: something is wrong here. One has to wonder whatever became of the Blessed Alliance we read about in Genesis and that Jesus recovered among his disciples.

A LOPSIDED RATIO IN THE CHURCH

These issues took on global implications as I prepared for a women's conference in Sasebo, Japan. Never having set foot on Japanese soil, I decided I'd better bone up on the world of Japanese women. I picked up the phone and started calling people—mostly missionaries—who had spent time in Japan and might be able to help me. I heard the same story everywhere I turned. The Japanese church is very small. Christians make up one-third of 1 percent of the Japanese population. Within the churches, women outnumber men two to one, and in many congregations the female majority is vastly larger. But instead of rejoicing that God is building his church in Japan, this last statistic is often accompanied by a degree of hand-wringing over the shortage of men in the church. While everyone would like to see more Japanese men become Christians, it is as if the church is somehow hampered with so many women and so few men. I often wonder how these sentiments sound to faithful, hard-working, serious-minded Japanese women.

In the New Testament you don't find the same kind of hand-wringing when the scales tilted in favor of women in Philippi. This apparent lack of concern is especially surprising considering the fact that the apostle Paul was involved. Anyone who knows anything about Paul would expect him to wring his hands over what happened in Philippi. A pureblooded Jew with the pedigree to prove it, Paul was a former Pharisee purist when it came to the letter of the law. As an apostle of Jesus Christ, Paul's admonitions for women to wear veils and to keep silent in the church have stirred up no end of controversy and convinced his critics that Paul was no advocate for women. One critic even went so far as to label the great apostle "the prophet of female inferiority," an impression fueled by some of the church's leading theologians (men as significant as St. Augustine) who interpreted Paul to be saying women weren't made in the image of God as fully as men were—something Paul didn't intend and Genesis refutes.

To make matters worse, the unmarried Paul was an outspoken enthusiast for the single life. According to the apostle, marriage and children would bog him down and prevent him from freely doing the work of the Lord. Having been single for a number of years, I applaud his high view of singles and appreciate the freedom a single person has for ministry. Still, as a wife, it feels a little strange to think of marriage as an encumbrance. Given Paul's background and reputation as a hard-liner when it comes to women in the church, he seems like the last apostle to send into a situation involving women. Then again, his single status made him the perfect candidate to show the world that God calls every man—single or married—to join with women in the Blessed Alliance.

Despite Paul's reputation, the Holy Spirit drafted him for the Philippi assignment, even interrupting him midway through his strategically important second missionary journey (Acts 16:6–40). Accompanied by Silas, Timothy, and Luke, Paul was revisiting and fortifying fledgling churches he and Barnabas had planted in Asia Minor (today's Turkey) on their first missionary expedition. He carefully mapped out his itinerary for this crucial follow-up journey so they could make the most of their time on the road.

Plans fell through abruptly when the Holy Spirit somehow blocked their path and then, through a vivid dream, redirected them to Macedonia (modern Greece). In the vision, Paul saw a Macedonian man standing and pleading urgently, "Come over to Macedonia and help us" (Acts 16:9). What a thrilling moment! God was opening the door to Europe—a historic development. The apostle canceled all other plans. His team packed for an immediate departure and set sail for Europe. They didn't stop until they reached Philippi, a major Roman colony and a leading metropolis in that region of Macedonia.

Expectations were surely riding high. Nothing quite like this had ever happened before. I've never had a vision, but if I had one like Paul's, I'd be anticipating major revival, perhaps a stadium packed with people on the edge of their seats eagerly waiting for the first strains of "Just As I Am." What Paul and his cohorts found at the end of the road was nothing like that, although, upon reflection, it was no less extraordinary. Instead of a stadium of people eager to hear and respond to the gospel, Paul found a group of women praying outside the city gate, along the river-bank. If Paul was disappointed, the text does not say. But, clearly, God intended to establish a beachhead for the gospel in Enemy territory on European soil with a band of women.

THE FOUNDING MOTHERS OF PHILIPPI

Whatever Paul and Silas were thinking at the time, they didn't let on. Instead, they sat down and began speaking about Jesus to the women who had gathered, as though meeting with a group of women was an everyday occurrence. What makes this encounter even more remarkable is the fact that these women were Gentiles, not Jewish insiders like Mary Magdalene and the other Galilean women who followed Jesus. Evidently they had heard about the God of Abraham from Jewish exiles in Philippi and, as a result, had become "God fearers." They didn't yet know about Jesus. Paul found them on the Sabbath worshiping and praying to Isra-el's God at a place of prayer outside the city gates. In all probabil-ity, the women were meeting at the river because in Philippi there was no Jewish synagogue. According to Jewish law, a quorum of ten men was necessary to establish an official synagogue. It seems incredible (even slightly amusing) when you think about it—for a former Jewish Pharisee and religious terrorist to be sitting on the riverbank teaching Gentile women about Jesus on a Sabbath afternoon. Surely this is a sign of the transforming power of the gospel in a man's life.

Lydia, a successful businesswoman, was first to respond to the gospel. She's best remembered as a dealer in purple cloth she imported from Asia. Luke, who was with Paul at the time and recorded these events, confirmed that Lydia was at least part of the reason they had come. "The Lord opened her heart to respond to Paul's message" (Acts 16:14). As with any true conversion, Lydia's faith in Christ immediately led to action as she opened her home to shelter and care for the apostles. According to Luke's account, this was more than a polite gesture. She insisted they stay with her. The *ezer*-warrior emerges almost immediately in Lydia. Despite the threat of danger to herself, she never retracted her offer. By the time hostilities forced the apostles out of Philippi, Lydia's home appears to be the established meeting place for the Philippian church (Acts 16:40).[1] This wasn't the last time Paul benefited from Philippian determination, courage, and generosity.

If the apostles felt concern over the shortage of men, things only went from bad to worse. Paul was drawn into an incident involving a young slave girl possessed by an evil spirit who was enriching her owners by telling fortunes. Day after day, she kept following and harassing the apostles until Paul could stand it no longer. He turned around and cast out the evil spirit. It was almost certainly the case that the female count in the Philippian church increased by one. If she came to faith in Christ, you can be sure there was rejoicing in heaven. But was there rejoicing on earth? Or did the bewildered apostles mutter under their breath, "Not another woman"?

The demon-possessed girl's owners were outraged at losing their source of income. They retaliated by seizing Paul and Silas and dragging them to the authorities. Instead of facing a lawsuit, the apostles were stripped, "severely flogged," and thrown into prison, where they suffered insomnia and the added trauma of an earthquake so severe it broke open the prison doors. The whole nightmarish ordeal was an eye-opener for these new Philippian converts. Instead of ushering in the good life, faith in Jesus was making everything worse. Yet amazingly, events that should have snuffed out the gospel in Philippi were actually demonstrating its power. Even the biggest optimist among these new believers was stunned to learn the crisis had brought the Philippian jailer to his knees and that, after turning to Christ, this tough, hardened man gently bathed the apostles' wounds, took them into his home, and served them a meal. The Philippians were witnessing with their own eyes the power of Jesus Christ to transform lives and to gain ground against the Enemy even under the worst of circumstances.

After the earthquake, city officials demanded that Paul and Silas leave Philippi. But the seed they had sown had taken root and was already sprouting. There may not have been enough Jewish men in Philippi to form an official synagogue, but the apostle Paul established one of the leading New Testament churches with a group of women.[2] This groundbreaking development for the gospel was decidedly female. A woman was the first convert to Christianity in Europe, and the first church plant in Europe was predominantly female. Paul had crossed a cultural divide, but in doing so he was only following the lead of Jesus.

One can only imagine Paul's frustration at having to abandon this infant church at such an early stage. He left behind a lot of unfinished business and a small army of new believers to carry on without him. He trusted God to finish the good work he had begun, although you can be sure that in Paul's pastor-heart he longed to have an active role. No one, least of all the apostle, anticipated how much God would do through these new Christians or the enormous impact this little church would have on Paul himself.

A LETTER FROM PRISON

Was Paul disappointed when the Holy Spirit led him to a group of praying women? Did he fear the feminization of the church in Philippi? Was he looking for a few good men to take over this new ministry that was overloaded with women? Had the Holy Spirit made some terrible mistake?

Some years[3] later, from a Roman prison cell, Paul gave his answer in a letter he wrote to his friends in Philippi. "I thank my God every time I remember you. In all my prayers for all of you, I always pray with joy because of your partnership in the gospel *from the first day* until now" (Philippians 1:3–5, emphasis added). As the Philippian believers read his letter aloud, they knew who Paul had in mind—the founding mothers of the Philippian church who partnered with him in the gospel "from the first day." Judging from his letter, that first day along the riverbank at Philippi proved to be an extraordinary blessing in Paul's life.

Many modern scholars believe Philippi was Paul's favorite church. This particular letter is a standout within the collection of his writings because it is unusually personal and affectionate. "I have you in my heart" (1:7). "God can testify how I long for all of you with the affection of Christ Jesus" (1:8). "You whom I love and long for, my joy and crown" (4:1). No other letter contains such warm words from Paul's pen. Based on the endearing expressions found in this letter, Paul clearly enjoyed a particular closeness with this group of believers that was distinct from other churches.

Evidently, looking back, Paul could see that the Holy Spirit redirected him to Philippi in part because the women there needed to hear the gospel and partly because *he* needed the ministries these women had to offer him. It appears the so-called "prophet of female inferiority" had a high regard for women after all and valued them as an invaluable gift from God because of their "partnership in the gospel from the very first day."

It is important to note that, when Paul directly addressed the women in his letter, he was underscoring the fact that his letter was intended for women as much as it was for men. The same is true of all New Testament writings, of course. The Bible doesn't distinguish a different brand of Christianity for women and another for men. But sometimes it's good to have an explicit reminder that biblical writers had women readers specifically in mind. When we read and study the Bible, we're not eavesdropping on what the apostles were writing to men. Women should read Paul's letter to the Philippians from start to finish with the understanding that every word he wrote was meant for us too. So, reading Paul's letter from a female point of view, what was Paul's message for women? How were women partners in the gospel with Paul?

CO-WARRIORS WITH THE APOSTLE

Paul valued women as his partners in battle. When hostilities erupted in Philippi and the apostles were driven out of town, members of this infant church didn't have the luxury of remaining on the sidelines. The battle was raging, and the Philippian Christians were called to stand against the Enemy. The women of Philippi did not excuse themselves from responsibility because they were "only women." This courageous band of *ezers* possessed the gospel and the responsibility both to live it out and to defend it. Paul was counting on them. "Their share or partnership in the gospel was not a quiet enjoyment of it, but a keen activity in the interest of it ... from the first time it was preached to them by Paul until now."[4]

Once a few more men came on the scene, some might expect Paul to instruct the women in Philippi to take a backseat in the church. Instead, in his letter he shows no sign of letting up or relieving women of their responsibilities. There's no hint of women carrying a lighter load or taking shelter from the heat of battle behind the men. He addressed men and women *together* with the same strong call to battle.

Paul knew exactly what he was doing when he employed military language when he wrote to the Philippian church. His warrior language was perfectly appropriate for women because God created women to be warriors. Reports that these *ezers* in Philippi were standing firm on their local battlefront energized Paul for the battles facing him. Their strong solidarity with him for the cause of Christ bolstered his morale and fueled his courage to fight on. As he told them all, both men and women, "We are in this fight together" (Philippians 1:30 NLT).

Paul regarded himself and the Philippians as co-warriors on different fronts of the same battle. Paul's battlefront was a Roman prison cell where the threat of death hung ominously over his head, jealous adversaries were seeking to intensify his sufferings, and chains prevented him from going to the churches that desperately needed his guidance. On the Philippian front, believers faced hostilities from pagan enemies on the outside, subversion from false teachers within, and divisive interpersonal conflicts among their ranks. These were not battles for men to fight while the women watched and prayed from a safe distance. He urged women to stand firm against the Enemy alongside their brothers, to join in the battle for the gospel, and to be on guard against false teaching. Paul held women, as well as men, responsible for protecting and maintaining the unity of the church. He urged the whole church to stand "side by side, fighting together for the Good News" (Philippians 1:27 NLT). Women were Paul's partners in battle.

CO-LABORERS FOR THE GOSPEL

Paul also valued women as his partners in ministry. Right from day one, women labored at his side to spread the gospel in Philippi. When he was driven out of town, they carried on the work in his absence without losing momentum. "Women seemed to have played a major role in the Philippian church, not only in meeting the physical needs of the missionaries, but also in working side by side with them in the proclamation of the gospel."[5] The church in Philippi grew because women were spreading the good news of Jesus Christ.

Paul named two women he considered indispensable to this crucial effort. Euodia and Syntyche were embroiled in a serious disagreement that was sidelining them from vital ministry and threatening the unity of the church (Philippians 4:2–3). You might think having your name show up in the Bible because you were having a quarrel to be a permanent source of embarrassment or, worse, to give evidence, as some have surmised, to the false notion that women are naturally more inclined to be quarrelsome than men. While Paul intended to correct and restore, he also meant to honor his two friends. His concern reflects their significance to him and their profound influence on the whole church.[6] In urging them to set aside their dispute for the sake of unity, he speaks of them with the utmost respect as "women who have contended [or labored] at my side in the cause of the gospel" (Philippians 4:3) — words that carry a metaphorical reference to gladiators fighting side by side in the arena. "It implies a united struggle in preaching the gospel, on the one hand, and sharing in the suffering that results from the struggle, on the other.... Paul wishes to say that these women are not in any way to be degraded for their disagreements, but to be respected highly for their energetic cooperation with him, working at his side as esteemed members of his team ... equal in importance to Clement and the rest of Paul's fellow laborers."[7] Far from demeaning women, Paul is actually declaring them essential for ministry. As the commanding general, Paul is admonishing two of his frontline soldiers to work together to advance the gospel.

MINISTRY TO THE APOSTLE

Even more remarkable, the Philippian women not only ministered *with* Paul, they ministered *to* him. They started ministering to him the second Lydia opened her home. Apparently they never stopped. The same Lydia-brand of dogged determination characterized the whole church's untiring efforts to assist Paul in his ministry. When he was driven out of Philippi, they followed him to Thessalonica, bringing gifts and aid (Philippians 4:16). Now, as the incarcerated Paul was writing this letter to dear friends back in Philippi, they were still at it, for next to him in the prison was a Philippian attending to his needs. Epaphroditus wasn't there on his own initiative. The Philippian church sent him as their representative. Though they were struggling back home to make ends meet, they generously loaded up Epaphroditus with supplies and explicit instructions to "take care of Paul," then sent him off to find the apostle. Although it cannot be demonstrated from the text, many believe Lydia's wealth was the primary source behind Epaphroditus's ministry to Paul. A driving force behind this mission to Paul was her heart for Christ and for his apostle's physical and spiritual needs, concerns deeply shared by her Philippian sisters in Christ.

Having grown up in a pastor's home and now as part of a seminary community, I have some idea of the constant burdens a pastor carries for his congregation. Whenever there's a problem in the church or someone is in trouble, the pastor's phone usually rings first, and he's forever getting under other people's burdens. Then, too, despite impressions to the contrary, a pastor has deep spiritual struggles of his own. Paul was no exception. His faith was constantly under fire. Discouragement and burnout were as much of a problem to him as to any overburdened pastor today. Even those Christians we regard as giants of faith are vulnerable and wrestle to trust God just like the rest of us when things are going badly. But it is rare, sad to say, for a pastor or a man of

Paul's stature in the Christian community to find a safe place to unburden himself and receive the spiritual encouragement and support he needs. In candid moments, a lot of pastors acknowledge their lives at times can be pretty lonely.

The Philippians broke that loneliness for Paul. I'm convinced the reason they reached out to him had a lot to do with the influence of women in the church. In his letter, he is uncharacteristically vulnerable, talking about himself, his circumstances, his adversaries, his fears, and his joy. The Philippians had already ministered to him and obviously opened the door for him to continue unburdening himself on them. They apparently made it clear they were interested in more than the latest missionary bulletin of activities and conversions. They wanted to know how *he* was doing in his heart through all the good and bad things that were happening to him. And so he opened up to them. It's impossible to quantify what it meant to have this group of believers praying fervently for him, tracking his movements, sharing his ups and downs, and relentlessly reaching out to minister to him. We feel the same way whenever we find someone willing to listen, someone with whom we can be open and honest about what is really going on inside us. Little wonder he thanked God for them.

One of the most heartening aspects of my speaking ministry is the opportunity to observe firsthand the rich spiritual ministries women offer the church. Women I meet all over the country are theologically astute, wise counselors, actively involved in each other's lives. Sometimes they get involved in my life too, and I am personally enriched and blessed by my sisters in the faith. I come away from women's conferences convinced that the church is sitting on a spiritual gold mine because of the gifts God has entrusted to women. What saddens me most is how few men there are who, like Paul, tap into this extraordinary vein of spiritual refreshment—for themselves. Pastors and other men in churches are pleased to have a strong women's ministry in their church.

They are rightfully delighted when women take a serious interest in studying the Bible and theology and desire to go deeper in their relationship with God. I am thankful for the many men who are thoughtful, interested advocates for women and their ministries. But do they realize their own need for the rich spiritual wisdom and encouragement that is flourishing right under their noses? Paul made that discovery. He valued the spiritual ministries of women to him and with him. This is as it should be, for even (perhaps especially) for a single man like the apostle Paul, "it is not good for the man to be alone."

PAUL'S MESSAGE FOR US

Judging from Paul's relationship with the Philippians, he is *not* against women. He is *for* women. He champions women as members of the body of Christ, as ministers of the gospel at his side, and as ministers to him personally. He wants them to stand with him in battle. He calls them to join him as kingdom builders in spreading the gospel and building up the church. He longs to be blessed and fortified by the spiritual ministries they offer. His views of women fit perfectly within the big picture that we have been seeing throughout the Bible. Paul's message for women is as radical, countercultural, and affirming as the rest of Scripture. His teachings, attitudes, and actions convey the most affirming message for women the world has ever known. Admittedly, Paul makes statements that are difficult to understand and which the church has fiercely debated over the years without reaching a consensus. But wherever one lands in the debate, Paul's appreciation for the women of Philippi cannot be denied.

Any woman in first-century Philippi reading Paul's letter picked up strong signals from the apostle that her gifts were vital to the cause of Christ. She learned from Paul that her actions impacted the spread of the gospel as well as the imprisoned apostle's morale. A lot was riding on whether she stood firm or held back.

Today, when we read Paul's letter to the Philippians—whether we are women living in Japan or North America or anywhere else—that same strong message reaches us. Paul wrote to a congregation of people he knew personally, but the Holy Spirit meant for his letter to fall into our hands too. It is not just a message for women. It is a message for the church.

I met a pastor who got the message and began taking concrete steps toward living in the light of Paul's teachings regarding women, starting with his own marriage. For years he had been laboring under the mistaken assumption that as pastor he was supposed to be taking care of everyone else—first and foremost his wife and children, but also the members of his congregation. But who was going to minister to him? Privately, he felt the weight of his own spiritual needs and was finding it hard to carry such a heavy load alone without the spiritual encouragement that we all need from other believers. Everything changed for him when he realized God intended for Christian women—*ezers*—to join their brothers as co-warriors and co-laborers for the gospel. I'll never forget his response. "I'm going home to ask my wife to forgive me. I've never thought of her as a spiritual resource to me."

Paul approached the question of the gifts and ministries of women from the same angle. His mission was the proclamation of Jesus Christ—a vast global enterprise calling for the full effort of all the troops. He longed to remain strong for the overwhelming battles he personally faced. He couldn't do any of this alone and wasn't shy about expressing how much he needed the ministries of the women who were there "on the first day." He called women, then and now, to join him in pouring out their lives for Christ and for his gospel. He valued their minds, their gifts, and their partnership in ministry. He was stronger in battle and in ministry because of the rich ministries of women with him and to him.

Paul wasn't trying to be progressive or to "get with the times." He was simply following a very old blueprint—the one God designed in the beginning and that Jesus revived in his ministry. It is still "not good for the man to be alone." God's remedy is still the same. He calls men and women to serve him together. When women's spiritual gifts and ministries are overlooked or underutilized, *both* men and women lose. According to Paul, the church is strongest and her burdens lighter when the Blessed Alliance is strong and men and women are pulling together in the same direction. Without this kind of unity, we are like a runaway carriage—going nowhere fast. When the team panics and pulls in different directions, disaster awaits everyone. But when we are side by side, shouldering the load together and pulling the church carriage forward in unity, God's image shines forth brightly in us, and we will advance God's kingdom in our generation.

So what have we learned from the lost women of the Bible? What do we take with us as we walk away from their stories? Before closing this book, let's take one final look together at these trusted old friends and their message for us.

FOCUS: The apostle Paul is often viewed as having negative views of women. But his relationship with the women of Philippi strongly contradicts that impression. We will see through Paul's close relationship with these first female converts in Europe how much our brothers need us and the vital part we play in advancing Christ's kingdom.

PAUL AND THE WOMEN OF PHILIPPI STORY:
Acts 16:6–40; Philippians 1–4

FOR DISCUSSION, READ: Philippians 1:1–11, 27–30

1. Does "two are better than one" describe your experience in working with men in marriage, the workplace, or in the church? Why or why not?

2. What has happened to the Blessed Alliance since the Fall? Why is this alliance so important?

3. The gospel of Jesus Christ not only changes us, it also changes our relationships, including relationships between men and women. How do we see that illustrated through Paul and his relationships with the women of Philippi? How was Paul a changed man?

4. Who was Paul referring to when he spoke of those who were there "on the first day," and why did he value the partnership of women with him in the gospel?

5. According to Genesis 1:26–28 and Matthew 28:18–20, what was the scope of the mission God entrusted to Paul and to the women of Philippi?

6. How were women standing with him in battle? Why was this so important to him?

7. How were they ministering to his physical and spiritual needs?

8. Why do men *need* the gifts God has entrusted to us? Why are *ezers* vital to the church?

CONCLUSION:
LOST AND FOUND

Even a cursory reading of Scripture reveals that God is looking for men."

As I read through an article designed to mobilize men for the gospel and for the church, that old lost feeling swept over me again. Not that I question the importance of men. To the contrary, my own "cursory reading" of the Bible tells me God is looking for men. Not only that, but without pausing to scratch my head or pensively chew the end of my pencil, I can produce a sizable list of men I know to make a strong case that God is *still* looking for men. My husband, my dad, my brothers and uncles, a lineup of Bible teachers, professors, and friends, and I'm just getting started. The article went on to say, "God is looking for men with humble hearts; men who will sacrifice anything for Christ and the advancement of His Kingdom."[1] I know a lot of men like that—lost men Jesus found and called to follow him. They obeyed his call. God's work in their lives spilled over into mine. It's a good thing God is looking for men.

At the same time, when I read something like this, I can't help wondering if the flip side of this statement is also true. Is God looking for women too? Women "with humble hearts ... who will sacrifice anything for Christ and the advancement of His Kingdom"? More than anything, I want to know for myself: Is God looking for me?

STRIKING GOLD FOR WOMEN AND FOR THE CHURCH

Even in our rapidly changing world, the Bible remains by far the best place for us to search for answers. A cursory reading of Scripture might not be enough to unearth the kinds of answers we seek, but as scholar Julia Neuberger assures us, "women's story is there written large, though it may be hidden in the text, and finding it might be like digging for gold."[2] There is gold for us in the lives of the lost women of the Bible and in their teachings about the God who relentlessly loves his daughters and who is counting on them to build his kingdom. So I pose the question to them, "Is God looking for women?" The answer is nested in their stories.

"Abraham, where is your wife, Sarah?" "Hagar, servant of Sarai, where have you come from, and where are you going?" "Esther, who knows but that you have come to royal position for such a time as this?" "God sent the angel Gabriel to Nazareth, a town in Galilee, to a virgin pledged to be married to a man named Joseph." "Mary, go and tell my brothers." "Paul, come over to Macedonia and help us!"

A *careful* reading of Scripture reveals that God *is* indeed looking for women—women "with humble hearts ... who will sacrifice anything for Christ and the advancement of His Kingdom." Lost women he found and called to follow him. They obeyed his call. God's work in their lives spills over into ours. It's a good thing God is looking for women.

WOMEN AS KINGDOM BUILDERS

Who would have guessed that God would do so much through the handful of women we have just considered? Or that today we would still be feeling the force of their influence? They may not get the same high level of coverage that went to some of the men in the Bible, but the power of their lives is as great and their godly influence is as lasting. Their individual stories revive my hope that in God's family, girls do count after all. Together these women from biblical times weave a powerful story that tells us God's hand is with his daughters, and they are strong for him. As warriors for his kingdom, they passed on to us a rich legacy, a vital mission God calls us to carry on.

God calls women to make crucial contributions in the shaping of his church. Women of old helped to lay the foundations of what Christians believe today. Through deeply personal struggles, women like Sarah, Hagar, and Hannah broke new ground in our understanding of God's character and his intimate involvement in our lives. They were early formulators of the theology of Israel and of the church today. Sarah offered living proof that *nothing* is too hard for the Lord and that he always keeps his promises, no matter how hopeless or impossible it may seem. Hagar introduced us to El Roi—the God who sees and cares for *me*—a truth Christians turn to again and again when they feel forgotten and insignificant. Hannah's psalm unveiled a God who rules over the ups and downs of life. She taught us to draw our strength and joy from God. Her theology fuels our faith by assuring us that God is advancing his purposes, even in the dark times of our lives. Hannah's wisdom gives us confidence that, whether we rise or fall, God holds us safely in his strong hands. Biblical writers would have left out major portions of the Scriptures without the collaborative efforts of Mary of Nazareth, Mary Magdalene, and other women who were eyewitnesses to the most significant events of Jesus' life.

God calls women to make his people strong too. Women of the Bible are pillars of strength to his church. What would Hagar think if she knew her private encounter with the Angel of the Lord and what she learned about his care for her was bolstering the faith of Christians thousands of years later? (What would Abraham and Sarah think?) No doubt Hannah would be gratified to discover the theology she drew out of the crucible of infertility and taught to her young son Samuel forms the bedrock of the church's theology. Kings, godly leaders, and stalwart martyrs like Paul and the young slave girl Blandina embraced Hannah's teaching that God's hand rules over all of life (from the cradle to the grave) and went to their deaths with courage. You can easily imagine the smile that would come over Esther's face if she heard that her spiritual fortitude in the face of genocide was still injecting courage into the veins of God's people so many generations later.

In keeping with his own declaration that "it is not good for the man to be alone," God also calls women to minister to men. He raised up women like Tamar, Hannah, and Esther to crucial places of leadership during perilous times when the purposes of God were under threat. God worked through these women as they used their wits and righteous influence — "as iron sharpens iron" — to honor their God, transform men's lives, and change the course of history. Who knows what comfort Jesus himself derived from the faithful band of women who had the spiritual stamina to remain with him throughout his crucifixion? What would the imprisoned Paul have missed, how would his sufferings have deepened, without the spiritual reinforcement that came from the persevering ministries of the women of Philippi?

God calls women to a purpose—revealed when he created Eve—that is unchanging and also expansive enough to encompass the whole of every woman's life. Our calling as *ezers* and image bearers starts when we start and can go with us anywhere God leads us, right down to the finish line. The dimensions of his blueprint, just in the lives of the few women we have studied, are simply breathtaking. Who would guess that the Bible's paradigm for women is big enough to suit a woman of power like Persia's Queen Esther as well as an Egyptian nobody like Hagar, Sarah's powerless slave girl? God's purposes made room for a little girl from Nazareth named Mary, who was just starting out in life and learning all she could about God, and also for the aging Sarah who, at the other end of life, had given up on any possibility that she could count for anything.

What is more, God recruits kingdom builders with all sorts of resumes. His purposes made powerful strides through the likes of a shrewd outsider like Tamar the Canaanite, the wise and gentle but socially discredited Hannah, and a deranged and resistant Magdalene, as well as through the sinful woman who repented and wept at his feet. He calls us all to follow him and lend our energies to his cause, no matter how lost we've been in the past.

Through the women of the Bible, God puts real everyday faith on display for the world to see. Their stories portray in vivid tones the resolute "risk it all" brand of courage that faith in such a God produces. Women as diverse as Sarah, Tamar, Mary of Nazareth, and many other strong women like them joined hands across the centuries to fight, even risk their lives, for the promised seed. The hope Eve lost in the Garden of Eden rested in Mary's arms in a Bethlehem stable. Hannah sacrificed everything for the honor of God's name. Esther risked her life to save his people. Their bravery and sacrifices should never be minimized. They offer powerful reminders that God is alive and well in the lives of his daughters, and women's efforts for his kingdom are vital.

SERVING GOD WHERE WE ARE

Probably most of us will spend our lives behind the scenes, like Mrs. Noah did. No one will remember our face or anything we did. Like Mrs. Noah, our stories won't get told, and our lives will be reduced to a few etchings — a name and a couple of dates — on a small headstone in a quiet cemetery. People who wander by from time to time will never know (and maybe we won't either) how much God accomplished through something we said or did or a life we touched in his name.

But our influence does live on, even though we are gone. Whatever we do for God's kingdom, whether we serve him in small ways or large, has lasting effects that will outlive us. God calls us to minister in his name to those around us, and he is building his kingdom through our efforts.

My friend Lilian tells me that lost feeling will be with us till Jesus comes. In my heart of hearts, I know she's right. Still there are days when that feeling evaporates — when a man like Judah steps up to the microphone and publicly acknowledges the righteousness of a woman's bold actions. Sometimes a Mordecai, a Joseph, or a Paul comes along who values our gifts, partners with us, and cheers us on as we serve God.

But even without their affirmation, that lost feeling has a hard time staying with us when we sense the smile of God as we walk with him and devote ourselves to his cause. He is El Roi, and his eye is always on us. We are his image bearers. We are *ezers*. We are vital members of the Blessed Alliance. We know our efforts matter to God and that our brothers need us now. We are women "with humble hearts ... who will sacrifice anything for Christ and the advancement of His Kingdom."

We follow Jesus, and no one who follows Jesus is lost.

FOCUS: The lost women of the Bible were never lost to God. We will reflect on what we have learned from their stories about God and about God's call on our lives as image bearers, *ezers*, and members of the Blessed Alliance.

FOR DISCUSSION, READ: Philippians 1:9–11, 27–30

1. What have you learned from the lost women of the Bible that changes how you see yourself?

2. How have you been helped because of their deep struggles with God? How has your vision expanded of yourself and of your mission as a kingdom builder?

3. Which woman do you think best fulfilled her calling to be God's image bearer and an *ezer*? Why?

4. What strong examples do these women give us of the Blessed Alliance, both in marriage and in other relationships between men and women?

5. How do these callings encompass the totality of every woman's life?

6. What does it mean for you to be God's image bearer today? What are the relationships where this calling is a challenge for you?

7. What people in your life need you to come alongside as the *ezer*-warrior to strengthen them in their walk of faith? What can we do to reactivate the Blessed Alliance in the church?

8. From what we have observed in the lives of these women, why is knowing God *central* to our callings as women and to our relationships with others?

Notes

Introduction: Lost

1. This life-changing struggle is the subject of my book *When Life and Beliefs Collide: How Knowing God Makes a Difference* (Grand Rapids, Mich.: Zondervan, 2001).
2. See Mark 7:31–37.
3. C. S. Lewis, *A Grief Observed* (New York: Bantam, 1961), 11.
4. J. I. Packer, *A Grief Sanctified: Passing Through Grief to Peace and Joy* (Ann Arbor, Mich.: Servant, 1997), 56.
5. Sheldon Vanauken, *A Severe Mercy* (New York: HarperCollins, 1980), 180.

Chapter 1: A Forgotten Legacy — Eve

1. Lilian Calles Barger, *Eve's Revenge, Women and a Spirituality of the Body* (Grand Rapids, Mich.: Brazos, 2003), 135.
2. Stanley J. Grenz, *Theology for the Community of God* (Nashville: Broadman & Holman, 1994), 224.
3. Eugene H. Peterson, *First and Second Samuel* (Louisville, Ky.: Westminster John Knox Press, 1999), 21.
4. In Genesis 2:18, *ezer* is modified by the Hebrew word *kenegdo*, which appears only in this passage and literally reads, "I will make for him a helper as in front of him (or according to what is in front of him)." Victor P. Hamilton, *The Book of Genesis Chapters 1–17, The New International Commentary on the Old Testament*, ed. R. K. Harrison (Grand Rapids, Mich.: Eerdmans, 1990), 175. According to Dr. Hamilton, "The new

creation will be neither a superior nor an inferior, but an equal. The
creation of this helper will form one-half of a polarity, and will be to man
as the south pole is to the north pole.... Any suggestion that this particular
word denotes one who has only an associate or subordinate status to a
senior member is refuted by the fact that most frequently this same word
describes Yahweh's relationship to Israel. He is Israel's help(er)."

5. *Ezer* is a military term, appearing twenty-one times in the Old Testament:
twice referring to the woman (Genesis 2:18 and 20); three times for military
powers Israel turned to for help (Isaiah 30:5; Ezekiel 12:14; Daniel 11:34);
the remaining sixteen occurrences refer to God as Israel's helper, each time
with military imagery (Exodus 18:4; Deuteronomy 33:7, 26, 29; Psalm
20:2; 33:20; 70:5; 89:19 (translated "strength" in the NIV); 115:9, 10, 11;
121:1–2; 124:8; 146:5; and Hosea 13:9.

6. For a more complete discussion of the *ezer*, see chapter 9 of my book *When
Life and Beliefs Collide: How Knowing God Makes a Difference* (Grand
Rapids, Mich.: Zondervan, 2001).

7. *Ezer* was also considered a fitting name to commemorate God's powerful
deliverance of the nation Israel. Samuel looked back on Israel's victories,
built a stone monument, and named it Eben-*ezer* to remind all Israel, "Thus
far has the LORD helped us" (1 Samuel 7:12).

8. See Genesis 3:1–6.

9. "She also gave some to her husband, *who was with her*, and he ate it"
(Genesis 3:6, emphasis added).

10. 1 Timothy 2:14.

11. Elizabeth Elliot, *Let Me Be a Woman* (Wheaton, Ill.: Tyndale, 1976), 25.

12. Proverbs 30:15–16.

13. See Gordon J. Wenham, *Genesis 1–15*, eds. David A. Hubbard and Glenn
W. Barker, vol. 1, *Word Biblical Commentary* (Waco, Texas: Word, 1987),
81.

CHAPTER 2: THE UNKNOWN SOLDIER — MRS. NOAH

1. Noah's wife is mentioned in Genesis 6:18; 7:7, 13; 8:16, 18.

2. Genesis 2:5.

CHAPTER 3: LIFE IN THE MARGINS — SARAH

1. Karen H. Jobes, *Esther, The NIV Application Commentary*, ed. Terry Muck
(Grand Rapids, Mich.: Zondervan, 1996), 128.

CHAPTER 4: THE INVISIBLE WOMAN — HAGAR

1. Richard Lacayo, "About Face: An Inside Look at How Women Fared under
Taliban Oppression and What the Future Holds for Them Now," *Time*
(December 3, 2001), 48.

2. Frederick Douglass, *My Bondage and My Freedom* (New York: Dover,
1969), 175.

3. Julius Lester, *To Be a Slave* (New York: Scholastic, 1968), 48–49.

4. Gordon J. Wenham, *Genesis 16–50, Word Biblical Commentary*, eds. David A. Hubbard and Glenn W. Barker (Dallas: Word, 1994), 8.

5. "Then Sarai said to Abram, 'You are responsible for the *wrong* [or *violence*] I am suffering. I put my servant in your arms, and now that she knows she is pregnant, she despises me. May the LORD judge between you and me'" (Genesis 16:5).

CHAPTER 5: MISSING IN ACTION — TAMAR

1. Matthew 1:1–17.

2. Michael Schuman, "Outward Bound," *Time* 163, no. 25 (June 21, 2004).

3. See Psalm 105:16–22.

4. Bruce K. Waltke, *Genesis* (Grand Rapids, Mich.: Zondervan, 2001), 513.

5. Wenham, 362; Victor P. Hamilton, *The Book of Genesis Chapters 18–50*, The New International Commentary of the Old Testament, ed. R. K. Harrison and Robert L. Hubbard Jr. (Grand Rapids, Mich.: Eerdmans, 1995), 446.

6. Paul twice exhorted *all* Christians to pursue a *quiet* or tranquil life (1 Thessalonians 4:11, 1 Timothy 2:2). Gentleness is required of church elders (1 Timothy 3:3). Paul himself was "*gentle* ... like a mother caring for her little children" in ministering to people (1 Thessalonians 2:7, emphasis added). But he also threatened to set aside his gentleness and use stronger measures when it came to flagrant disobedience among God's people (1 Corinthians 4:21). According to Paul, there's a time for gentleness and a time to be firm. A time to be quiet and a time to speak up.

CHAPTER 6: THE POWER BEHIND THE THRONE — HANNAH

1. Ben Carson, *The Big Picture: Getting Perspective on What's Really Important in Life* (Grand Rapids, Mich.: Zondervan, 1999), 107.

2. First Samuel 1:6 describes Peninnah as Hannah's "rival" wife or "one who vexes," which comes from a Hebrew root that "deals with the harassment and torment engendered by an enemy [or adversary].... Whenever a foe defeated Israel, he scoffed at Yahweh (Psalm 74:10, 23). So too the believer under oppression is taunted by his enemies. They ask, 'Where is your God?' (Psalm 42:10; cf. 31:11). In response the people entreated God to deliver them for the sake of his honor or reputation." *Theological Word Book of the Old Testament*, eds. R. Laird Harris, Gleason L. Archer, Jr., Bruce K. Waltke (Chicago: Moody Press, 1980), 2:779. Hannah's prayer of thanksgiving continues this theme as she celebrates the silencing of her enemy.

3. Instead of overruling her in this important spiritual and family matter, Elkanah deferred to her judgment and entrusted the matter to God. "Do what seems best to you ... only may the LORD make good his word" (1 Samuel 1:23).

4. Eugene H. Peterson, *First and Second Samuel* (Louisville, Ky.: John Knox, 1999), 24–25.

5. Both Hannah's prayers are psalms. The first is a lament, a cry of distress where Hannah lays her troubles before the Lord. She is desperate. No one

can help her except God alone. The second is a song of thanksgiving to God for answered prayer. For a helpful, easy-to-read treatment of Psalms, see Tremper Longman III, *How to Read the Psalms* (Downers Grove, Ill.: InterVarsity Press, 1988).

6. Eugene H. Peterson, *Answering God: The Psalms as Tools for Prayer* (San Francisco: HarperCollins, 1989), 15.

7. Carson, *The Big Picture*, 107.

8. Originally 1 and 2 Samuel formed a single volume. When the volume was translated from Hebrew into Greek, the length led translators to split the work in two. But 1 and 2 Samuel were intended to be read together as a single work.

9. Peterson, *First and Second Samuel*, 24, 13.

10. "Both compositions [1 Samuel 2:1–10 and 2 Samuel 22] rejoice in deliverance from enemies; celebrate God as a rock; speak of Sheol; and describe God's thundering in the darkness, his protection of the faithful, and his steadfast love for the Lord's anointed." Raymond B. Dillard and Tremper Longman III, *An Introduction to the Old Testament* (Grand Rapids, Mich.: Zondervan, 1994), 141.

11. C. S. Lewis, *A Grief Observed* (New York: Bantam, 1961), 73.

CHAPTER 7: A SLEEPING BEAUTY — ESTHER

1. Frederick Buechner, *Telling Secrets: A Memoir* (New York: HarperSanFrancisco, 1991), 17–18.

2. Frederic Bush, *Ruth/Esther*, eds. David A. Hubbard and Glenn W. Barker, *Word Biblical Commentary*, vol. 9 (Waco, Texas: Word, 1996), 355.

3. Jon D. Levenson, *Esther: A Commentary*, eds. James L. Mayes, Carol A. Newsom, and David L. Petersen, *The Old Testament Library* (Louisville, Ky.: Westminster John Knox Press, 1997), 47.

4. Some scholars believe by complying, Vashti would have lowered herself to the rank of a common concubine.

5. Ezra 9–10.

6. Leland Ryken, *Words of Delight: A Literary Introduction to the Bible* (Grand Rapids, Mich.: Baker, 1992), 118.

7. Karen Jobes, *Esther*, ed. Terry Muck, *The NIV Application Commentary* (Grand Rapids, Mich.: Zondervan, 1999), 120–21. The conflict between Haman and Mordecai goes back to the earliest days in Israel's history as a nation. "The Amalekites were a nomadic people of the southern desert region who frequently raided Israel from the beginning of its history. This heathen nation had the dubious distinction of being the first people of the world to attack and try to destroy God's newly formed covenant nation. Because of this, God promised Moses that he would completely erase the memory of the Amalekites from under heaven and would be at war with them from generation to generation (Ex. 17:8–16)."

By identifying Mordecai as "a Jew of the tribe of Benjamin" and a descendant of Kish (King Saul's tribe and his father), the narrator causes his first readers (the Israelites) to connect the story of Mordecai with Israel's first king. Agag was the king of the Amalekites at the time of Saul (1 Samuel 15), and God instructed Saul to utterly destroy Agag and the Amalekite nation. Instead, Saul spared the king and the best of the Amalekite livestock. It led to Saul's downfall.

By calling Haman "the Agagite," the narrator "is characterizing him as anti-Semitic, an enemy of the Jews. The original readers would have understood this one clue as introducing yet another episode of the age-old conflict between Israel and the powers that sought to destroy her."

8. No one knows what Mordecai meant when he told Esther she wouldn't survive either. Some think he was threatening to disclose her cover-up. Given his consistent protectiveness of her, this seems unlikely. There may have been government records—documentary proof of true citizenship and/or lists of aliens—that Haman and his supporters would research to root out every single Jewish person. It is also possible that Mordecai was warning Esther that to turn a blind eye to the extermination of God's people is to side with the enemy and put herself under God's curse: "I will bless those who bless you, and whoever curses you I will curse" (Genesis 12:3).

9. Bush, *Ruth/Esther*, 320.

10. Ibid., 321.

Chapter 8: The First Disciple—Mary of Nazareth

1. Eusebius, *The History of the Church*, trans. G. A. Williamson, ed. Andrew Louth, (London: Penguin, 1989), 141.

2. Ibid.

3. Timothy George, "The Blessed Evangelical Mary: Why we shouldn't ignore her any longer," *Christianity Today* (December 2003): 37.

4. Ruth Bell Graham, *Prodigals and Those Who Love Them* (Grand Rapids, Mich.: Baker, 1991), 50.

5. In Jesus' day, a common teaching method was for students to ask and answer questions. Jesus was a student here, interacting with the teachers, who were amazed at the questions and answers that were coming from this twelve-year-old boy.

6. Matthew's gospel provides the legal proof that Jewish people required to establish that Jesus was heir to David's throne through his adoptive father, Joseph (Matthew 1:1–17); Luke documents Jesus' physical lineage through his mother Mary's father, Heli. Both lines lead to King David (Luke 3:23–37).

7. Some additional examples of addressing a woman simply as "woman" are found in John 4:21, 8:10, and 20:13, 15.

8. The special relationship between Jesus and his mother and her knowledge of his true identity as the promised Messiah prompted her to make this request of her son. Commenting on Jesus' response to his mother, "Woman, what have I to do with you?" theologian Herman Ridderbos remarks, "Although in itself it need not contain anything offensive, materially it has the intent of a sharp reprimand. The fact that Jesus addresses it to his mother serves to show how much is at stake for him here. And it is precisely in regard to her that he had to observe sharply the boundaries of his authority (cf. Lk. 2:49f.)." Herman Ridderbos, *The Gospel of John: A Theological Commentary* (Grand Rapids, Mich.: Eerdmans, 1997), 105.

9. See Genesis 3:15.

1. Some attribute this confusion of Mary Magdalene with the sinful woman in Luke's gospel to a sermon preached in 591 by Pope Gregory the Great, although it is also possible that the close proximity of the stories of the two women in the Bible has caused people to assume they refer to the same woman. Some have also confused Mary of Bethany, the sister of Martha and Lazarus, with Mary Magdalene. The biblical text, however, clearly portrays the women as three separate individuals and gives no support for confusing them.

2. Gnostic gospels were a collection of writings and viewpoints written in the second century that were never part of the New Testament canon. They contain teachings that are a mingling of oriental religion, Christianity, and Greek philosophy. Their teachings were not uniform, although in general they taught that matter was evil and spirit was good and that salvation depended on possessing special knowledge, or gnosis.

3. For a response to Brown's assertions in *The Da Vinci Code*, see Darrell L. Bock, *Breaking The Da Vinci Code* (Nashville, Tenn.: Nelson, 2004).

4. Lists of women who followed Jesus: Matthew 27:55–56, 61; 28:1; Mark 15:40–41, 47; 16:1; Luke 8:1–3; 24:10; and John 19:25.

5. Ben Witherington III, *Women in the Ministry of Jesus: A Study of Jesus' Attitudes to Women and Their Roles as Reflected in His Earthly Life*, Society for New Testament Studies, gen. ed. G. N. Stanton (Cambridge, England: Cambridge University Press, 1984), 117.

6. Several of these women were wives or mothers of male disciples, Mary the mother of James and Joses, and the mother of James and John, for example. At least occasionally and certainly at the last, Jesus' mother was with him. The Gospels offer us no hint of Mary Magdalene's age, physical appearance, or station in life. The default view is that she was young and beautiful, but the Bible doesn't give any evidence to support that view. She could just as easily have been older, past child-bearing years, and delivered from demon possession too late in life to be considered marriageable.

7. Ruth A. Tucker and Walter Liefeld, *Daughters of the Church: Women and Ministry from New Testament Times to the Present* (Grand Rapids, Mich.: Zondervan, 1987), 29.

8. "Then Simon Peter, who had a sword, drew it and struck the high priest's servant, cutting off his right ear.... Jesus commanded Peter, 'Put your sword away! Shall I not drink the cup the Father has given me?'" (John 18:10–11).

9. Matthew 27:56 identifies the "other" Mary as "the mother of James and Joses."

10. See 1 Corinthians 15:12–20.

11. In an Easter sermon, St. Augustine noted how appropriate it was for Jesus to choose a woman to be first to proclaim his resurrection: "Because mankind fell through the female sex, mankind was restored through the female sex; because a virgin gave birth to Christ, a woman proclaimed that he had risen again. Through a woman death, through a woman life." Augustine, Sermon 232, *Sermons Part III, vol. 7 on the Liturgical Seasons*, trans. Edmund Hill, O.P., ed. John E. Rotelle, *The Works of Saint*

Augustine: A Translation for the 21st Century (New Rochelle, N.Y.: New City, 1997).

12. It is generally recognized by evangelical scholars that the New Testament uses the title *apostle* in two ways: first, to refer to the office held by Jesus' twelve male disciples and the apostle Paul, and second, in a looser sense, for individuals such as Barnabas, Epaphroditus, Apollos, Silvanus, and Timothy, who were messengers of the gospel. Mary was an apostle in this second, broader sense. See Douglas Moo, *The Epistle to the Romans*, *The New International Commentary on the New Testament* (Grand Rapids, Mich.: Eerdmans, 1996), 923–24.

   Historically the label "apostle to the apostles" for Mary Magdalene goes back to the third century, at least, and was a designation ascribed to her by church fathers. In his commentary on the Song of Songs, early church father Hippolytus, bishop and martyr of Rome around the year 235, refers to the women who were the first witnesses of the resurrection of Jesus as the "female apostles." Hippolytus described Jesus saying to the male apostles, "It is I who appeared to these women and I who wanted to send them to you as apostles" (Hippolytus, *De Cantico*, in *Corpus Scriptorum Christianorum Orientalium*, vol. 264 [Louvain, 1965], 43–49, translated by Katherine Ludwig Jansen in "Maria Magdalena: Apostolorum Apostola," in *Women Preachers and Prophets Through Two Millennia of Christianity*, eds. Beverly Mayne Kienzle and Pamela J. Walker [Berkeley, Calif.: University of California Press, 1998], 58). Evidently, the designation "apostle to the apostles" for Mary Magdalene caught on during the twelfth century (Jansen, "Maria Magdalena," *Women Preachers*, 69–71). Well-known biblical commentator Matthew Henry accorded the accolade to Mary Magdalene in his commentary on John's gospel. Remarking on John 20:17, he concluded, "She [Mary Magdalene] became the apostle to the apostles" (Matthew Henry, *Matthew Henry's Commentary on the Whole Bible*, vol. V [New York: Fleming H. Revell, 1900], 1215).

13. A. Moody Stuart, *The Three Marys: Mary of Magdala, Mary of Bethany, Mary of Nazareth* (Carlisle, Penn.: Banner of Truth, 1984), 75.

CHAPTER 10: RECOVERING THE BLESSED ALLIANCE — PAUL AND THE WOMEN OF PHILIPPI

1. In addition to Lydia, other women are identified as having hosted churches in their homes: Priscilla (Romans 16:3–5; 1 Corinthians 16:19), Nympha (Colossians 4:15), and possibly Chloe (1 Corinthians 1:11).

2. "Certainly it is clear from the Acts account that women played a noteworthy role in the founding and establishing of the Macedonian Churches (Acts 16:14, 40; 17:4, 12)." Jac J. Müller, *The Epistles of Paul to the Philippians and to Philemon*, gen. ed. F. F. Bruce, *The New International Commentary on the New Testament* (Grand Rapids, Mich.: Eerdmans, 1976), 179.

3. Scholars can't agree on when Philippians was written because they aren't sure to which imprisonment Paul refers in this letter. However, assuming that Paul's first visit to Philippi was roughly between AD 49–52 (according

to Dr. Gerald F. Hawthorne's best guess that Philippians was written from Caesarea somewhere around AD 62–63), approximately one decade elapsed between the "first day" and when Paul wrote the epistle to the Philippians. Gerald F. Hawthorne, *Philippians*, gen. eds., David A. Hubbard and Glen W. Barker, *Word Biblical Commentary* (Waco, Texas: Word, 1983), xliii–xliv.

4. Jac J. Müller, *The Epistles of Paul to the Philippians and to Philemon*, gen. ed. F. F. Bruce, *The New International Commentary on the New Testament* (Grand Rapids, Mich.: Eerdmans, 1976), 40.

5. Hawthorne, *Philippians*, xxxv.

6. Paul exhibits the same esteem for women as co-laborers for the gospel in the conclusion to his epistle to the Romans, where he identifies a number of women who worked hard and risked their lives alongside Paul and other men in the church. See Romans 16.

7. Müller, *The Epistles of Paul to the Philippians and to Philemon*, 180.

Conclusion: Lost and Found

1. J. P. Jones, "Where are the men?", www.pastors.com/article.asp?ArtID=5720, accessed July 5, 2005.

2. Michelle Guinness quoting Julia Neuberger in *Is God Good for Women?* (London: Hodder & Stoughton, 1997), 4.

When Life and Beliefs Collide

How Knowing God Makes a Difference

Carolyn Custis James

Sooner or later, life's difficulties bring every Christian woman to God's doorstep with questions too personal to ignore. "Why does God let me go through such painful circumstances?" "Why does he seem indifferent to my prayers?" We're tired of spiritual pie in the sky. We want authentic, God-as-he-really-is faith—the kind that holds us together when our world is falling apart and equips us to offer strength and hope to others.

When Life and Beliefs Collide raises a long-overdue call for us to think seriously about what we believe about God. With passion, brilliance, and eloquence, Carolyn Custis James weaves stories of contemporary women with episodes from the life of Mary of Bethany to illustrate the practical benefits of knowing God deeply. Examining the misperceptions and abuses that discourage women from pursuing a deeper understanding of God, this insightful book demonstrates how practical and down to earth knowing God can be.

> "There are few books that I feel every pastor should read, but this is one of them. Carolyn James originally wrote it for women to grow deeper with God, but men should read this book too. It is rich with insight for all of us."
>
> **—Rick Warren, Author of *The Purpose Driven® Life***

> "This outstanding book offers the best demonstration that everyone needs theology, the best expository account of Mary and Martha, and the best trajectory for women's ministry in modern North America that I have yet read."
>
> **—James I. Packer**

Softcover: 978-0-310-25014-2